LIFE

Our
Century
in Pictures

For Young People

LIFE

OUR
CENTURY
IN PICTURES

For Young People

Edited by Richard B. Stolley

Adapted by Amy E. Sklansky

LITTLE, BROWN AND COMPANY · BOSTON NEW YORK LONDON

CONTENTS

EDITOR'S NOTE: Dust Bowls and Other Dreams   vi

1900—1913: ACROSS THE THRESHOLD   1
"The Dawn of the American Century" by Katherine Paterson   2
TURNING POINT: *Titanic* and Beyond   19
REQUIEM: Mark Twain, Harriet Tubman, Geronimo, Susan B. Anthony   21

1914—1919: THE WAR TO END ALL WARS   23
"A New Kind of War" by Jane Yolen   24
TURNING POINT: The American Musical   33
REQUIEM: Buffalo Bill, Booker T. Washington, Pierre-Auguste Renoir, Frank Woolworth . . .   43

1920—1929: ALL THAT GLITTERS   45
"Get Hot!" by Avi   46
TURNING POINT: Closing the Gender Gap   53
REQUIEM: Lizzie Borden, Enrico Caruso, Wyatt Earp, Alexander Graham Bell . . .   63

1930—1939: EMPTY POCKETS   65
"Years of Hilarity and Heartbreak" by Robert Cormier   66
TURNING POINT: The Fugitive Kind   77
REQUIEM: Thomas Edison, Amelia Earhart, Sigmund Freud, George Gershwin . . .   89

1940-1945: WORLD ON FIRE   91

"The Home Front" by Lois Lowry   92

TURNING POINT: Conquest of the Atom   115

REQUIEM: Beatrix Potter, Lou Gehrig, F. Scott Fitzgerald, George Washington Carver . . .   119

1946-1963: SPREADING THE WEALTH   121

"Changes" by Patricia and Fredrick McKissack   122

TURNING POINT: Struggle for Respect   139

REQUIEM: Robert Frost, James Dean, Eva Perón, Frank Lloyd Wright . . .   155

1964-1975: DISSENT AND DISOBEDIENCE   157

"Years of Turbulence" by Jerry Spinelli   158

TURNING POINT: Exploring the Heavens   175

REQUIEM: Roberto Clemente, Che Guevara, Oskar Schindler, J. R. R. Tolkien . . .   183

1976-1992: A GLOBAL BURST OF FREEDOM   185

"Liberty for All" by Gary Paulsen   186

TURNING POINT: Shrinking the World   197

REQUIEM: Bob Marley, Dr. Seuss, Alfred Hitchcock, Jim Henson . . .   209

1993-1999: OurFuture.com   213

"Good Wins Out" by Cynthia Rylant   214

TURNING POINT: Origin of the Species   223

REQUIEM: Jerry Garcia, John F. Kennedy Jr., Arthur Ashe, Mother Teresa . . .   228

Index to Pictures   230

DUST BOWLS AND OTHER DREAMS

by Richard B. Stolley, Editor

In 1999, while everyone else was looking forward to the new century, those of us who produced this book were looking back intently at the old one.

This book is the result, a photographic history of the past 100 years. Our book has important words, of course — nine reflective essays by distinguished authors and informative captions for the nearly 400 pictures. But we wanted the photographs themselves to tell you the story of the fascinating century that just ended.

From them, we hope you will be able to see what famous people and historic events looked like, and thus understand better how your parents and grandparents and other relatives lived. We hope the pictures will help you realize how members of your family, going all the way back to 1900, were affected and influenced by the amazing things you will find in this book.

We have divided the book into nine chapters, nine groups of years. Within each chapter is a special section called Turning Point, where we look at a major news event — like the discovery of atomic power — and show what it meant to the rest of the century. And at the end of each chapter is another section called Requiem, in which we tell about some important people who died during those years. For example, did you know that the man who invented the game of basketball, James Naismith, lived from 1861 until 1939?

Deciding which pictures to use in our book, and which to leave out, was a very difficult job. We figure we looked at a grand total of 50,000 photographs from all over the world. As editor of the book, I spent every day looking at those pictures — and, to my surprise, dreaming about them at night. One night I dreamed I was an American soldier (called a doughboy) in France during World War I; another night, I was a farmer driving my family to California for a new life after a terrible drought had turned my Oklahoma fields into a dust bowl. I don't expect you to have such dreams, but I hope history will come alive for you as it did for me.

From looking at all those pictures, we understood clearly how violent the 20th Century had often been. But we also discovered again and again what a poet once described as "acts of kindness and of love," not to mention astonishing progress in medicine, science and the arts.

Personally, this book is a look back at my career as a journalist. I covered some of the history pictured here, such as the struggle for civil rights in the South, the war between the Arabs and Israelis, Elvis Presley in his early days as a rock 'n' roll star, angry students rioting in Paris, President John F. Kennedy's assassination in Dallas, the search for evidence in Africa of what life was like millions of years ago. I still have a handful of ancient crocodile bones that I found on that assignment — and a lot of memories from the others.

I hope this book will be for you, as it has been for me, a keepsake, a guide to the century that you lived in for a few years. If you understand the 20th Century better, I think, you will appreciate and enjoy the 21st Century even more.

I'd like to make one final point. While so much of the world suffered unprecedented death and destruction in the past 100 years, the United States was incredibly fortunate. We were largely spared. Our soldiers died in wars, but not our civilians. Our cities were not bombed; we were not invaded by foreign troops. Since the end of the Civil War in 1865, Americans have not gone into battle against other Americans. Those long-ago, cruel years of slavery still haunt us, but in our country today, we are mostly at peace.

This is worth remembering about America in the 20th Century: God indeed shed his grace on us, from sea to shining sea.

Joining Life *magazine in 1953, Richard B. Stolley served as chief of its bureaus in Atlanta, Los Angeles, Washington and Paris, and later as its editor. He was founding editor of* People *magazine in 1974 and then editorial director of the parent company, Time Inc., for which he is now senior editorial adviser.*

Reporting on the U.S. nuclear submarine base at Holy Loch, Scotland, in late March 1969, Dick Stolley, 41, was photographed on the deck of a sub about to embark on a 90-day Cold War patrol mission. He recalls, "Everyone topside was required to wear a life jacket because the wind — which the sailors called 'the hawk' — was strong enough to blow you overboard."

BILL RAY / LIFE

1900–1913

Up, up and away! Wilbur Wright, 35, piloted a glider above North Carolina in 1902. Next challenge for him and kid brother Orville: powered flight.

THE DAWN OF THE AMERICAN CENTURY

by Katherine Paterson

A new century seems full of hope and promise, like a new beginning for the world. The photograph of Wilbur Wright soaring above the sand dunes of Kitty Hawk in the plane he and his brother have made is a proper emblem for the excitement and promise of this century at its birth. While the picture of the mighty *Titanic*, all its lights ablaze, plunging prow first into the icy North Atlantic, cries out a warning. Look what disasters can occur, it seems to say, when technology is controlled by the arrogant and the greedy.

The 20th Century has been called the American Century. The 19th Century surely belonged to the expanding empires of Western Europe. No country in Asia, Latin America or Africa was safe from their colonizing greed. The young America, however, had a continent to conquer and a civil war to fight. It did not begin to look overseas until almost the end of that century. In rapid succession, Hawaii was annexed and the Philippines were taken over. President William McKinley declared in 1898:

"In a few short months, we have become a world power, and I know sitting here in this chair, with what added respect the nations of the world now view the United States . . . it is vastly different from the conditions I found when I was inaugurated."

Americans liked the idea of being a world power. The election of 1900 gave McKinley a second term. His vice-president was the young governor of New York State. Theodore Roosevelt was the sickly son of a wealthy New York family who, at the age of 25, had gone to the Badlands of North Dakota for his health and, he said, to shoot a buffalo while there were still one or two left to shoot. In two weeks' time he had fallen in love with the West, and he returned to New York with a love for the outdoors that never left him. When, a few months later, his young wife and his mother both died on the same day, he returned to his beloved Badlands for healing, dividing his time during the next two years between the rough existence of a North Dakota cattle rancher and the genteel life of a New York aristocrat. At the end of this period he was a new man physically and mentally. He settled in New York, married a childhood friend and turned his vast energy toward politics, a career interrupted only by his well-publicized exploits as Colonel Roosevelt, leader of the legendary Rough Riders and hero of the Spanish-American War.

When McKinley was assassinated less than a year after his inauguration, an appalled Republican political boss exclaimed: "Now look! That damned cowboy is president!"

Few American presidents have had as much effect on history as Teddy Roosevelt. (Yes, those teddy bears we all used to cuddle are his namesakes.) Defying the powerful interests of his own party, Roosevelt declared war on the so-called robber barons, especially J. P. Morgan and John D. Rockefeller, who had amassed enormous personal fortunes in oil and mining and railroads while abusing the environment and running roughshod over their workers.

His love of the wilderness and respect for ordinary citizens made him a pioneer conservationist, believing as he did that the forests, waters and natural resources of the nation belonged to all the people and that it was the role of government to protect and regulate their use on the people's behalf.

At the same time, Roosevelt believed in a powerful America that should not hesitate to make its weight felt internationally. "Speak softly," he said, "and carry a big stick." He didn't hesitate to tell Germany or France what they could or could not do in Latin America or Africa. In 1908, after seven years in the presidency, he received the Nobel Peace Prize for mediating an end to the war between Japan and Russia.

Perhaps most significantly, Roosevelt helped

TRAGEDY HITS

At 2:18 A.M. on April 15, 1912, a little more than two and a half hours after hitting the iceberg, the bow-flooded *Titanic* began its plunge to the bottom of the North Atlantic off the coast of New foundland. Seven hundred aboard escaped. Fifteen hundred did not.

KEN MARSCHALL / MADISON PRESS

bring about the new nation of Panama. His motives were soon clear. What he wanted was rights to a zone through which he could begin building his "big ditch." The Panama Canal was opened in 1914 and remained under American control until 1999.

To the relief of the rich and powerful, Roosevelt chose not to run for re-election in 1908. Rumor has it that when old J. P. Morgan heard that his enemy had sailed for Africa to hunt big game, he said: "Let every lion do his duty."

While Teddy Roosevelt was securing the nation's position in the world, American inventors were hard at work changing the nature of that world. The automobile, which had begun bumping down European and American roads in the 19th Century, was a toy of the rich until a young engineer named Henry Ford got the idea of an "assembly line" to mass-produce automobiles

FIRST FAMILY PHOTO

Moving into the White House with Teddy Roosevelt was the largest First Family ever. In this 1903 portrait, the President, then 44, posed with, from left: Quentin, 5; Theodore Jr., 16; Archibald, 9; Alice, 19; Kermit, 13; his second wife, Edith, 42; and Ethel, 12.

CORBIS / BETTMANN

cheaply enough for ordinary people to own them. Thomas Alva Edison was working away on inventions that would over his lifetime result in 1,093 patents. These would include the incandescent lightbulb, the phonograph and the movie camera. The Wright brothers were building powered aircraft. And although he didn't become an American citizen for another thirty years, a clerk in a Swiss patent office named Albert Einstein came up with a theory of relativity in 1905 that would revolutionize not only physics but the history of humankind.

History tends to remember the powerful and the great of any period, but photographs help us to remember the powerless. By the early 1900s, in all the industrialized nations, people were flocking to the cities to find work. In America, many of those people were immigrants, fleeing starvation

IN THE LINE OF DUTY

Having overseen the U.S.'s 1898 vanquishing of Spain (after which Cuba, Puerto Rico, Guam and the Philippines were handed over to the U.S.), William McKinley easily won a second term. He served only six months of it. On September 6, 1901, while visiting Buffalo, the 25th president became the third to be shot (after Lincoln and Garfield). McKinley, 58, lived eight more days; his assassin, 28-year-old anarchist Leon Czolgosz, lived another 53 days until he was sent to the electric chair.

TIME INC.

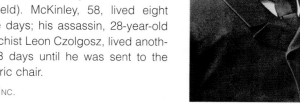

RICHEST MAN AROUND

The fortune amassed by J. P. Morgan, here with daughter Louisa and son J.P. Jr., would today trail only those of Bill Gates and Warren Buffet. He owned the U.S. Steel Corporation and built it into the world's largest corporation. Also among his holdings: railroads and England's White Star Line. In 1912, Morgan, 75, bought a ticket for *Titanic*'s maiden voyage but canceled at the last minute.

TIME INC.

or oppression. They came, mostly, to crowded city slums and went to work in dismal factories and sweatshops. Children were expected to help out their families, working under the same miserable conditions as their parents, whether in the fields or in the mills. There were very few health and safety regulations. Tragic accidents were all too common.

In the land of the free, most people did not enjoy the fruits of freedom. Susan B. Anthony and her companions in the women's suffrage movement had been fighting for the right to vote more than fifty years when Anthony died in 1906. It was another fourteen years before women were welcome at the ballot box. Harriet Tubman had led many of her fellow slaves out of bondage, but

when she died in 1913, equal rights for African-Americans remained only a distant dream.

When he realized that his successor, William Howard Taft, was either unwilling or unable to follow his dreams, Teddy Roosevelt declared himself a candidate for the presidency in 1912, but the party leaders had had enough of the "cowboy" who used what he called his "bully pulpit" to win the allegiance of the people and put pressure on politicians who disagreed with him. They chose the incumbent Taft as the Republican nominee. A stung Roosevelt gathered his supporters into a third party, which he called the Bull Moose. He made a strong showing, but the split Republican party lost to the Democratic candidate, Woodrow Wilson. A new chapter in the American Century had begun.

Winner of two Newbery Medals, a Newbery Honor, and the Hans Christian Andersen Award, Katherine Paterson is the author of many books for children and young adults. Her Newbery-winning classics are Bridge to Terabithia *and* Jacob Have I Loved. The Great Gilly Hopkins *was a Newbery Honor title and won both a National Book Award and a Christopher Award. Ms. Paterson's other books include National Book Award winner* Master Puppeteer, JIP, Flip-Flop Girl, *and* The Tale of the Mandarin Ducks.

MAJESTIC TWILIGHT

As the 20th Century dawned, four rulers — Queen Victoria, Tz'u-hsi, Nicholas II and Abdul Hamid II — governed three out of every five human beings alive. Their world was less populous (1.6 billion versus almost six billion now) and divided into fewer sovereign states (some 50 versus today's 190 plus). But their kingdoms, so dominant for centuries, were about to be engulfed by a global quest for independence. Revolutions swept out the Chinese and the Russian dynasties. Abdul Hamid II's Ottoman Empire crumbled after World War I. And in 1997, when Hong Kong was returned to China, the sun finally set on the British Empire.

NICHOLAS II

At 26, Nicholas II became the 18th in the Romanov royal family to rule Russia since 1613. He immediately took as his czarina Alexandra (right), a granddaughter of Queen Victoria. Comfortable only with his family and inner court, Nicholas was easily swayed by advisers like the mysterious and semiliterate faith healer Rasputin. Isolated from his subjects, he had no sense of the vast unrest that would lead to the Russian Revolution of 1917 — and to the violent end of his own life and the long Romanov reign (see page 34).

TIME INC.

TZ'U-HSI

No other concubine ever amassed the influence of China's notorious Empress Dowager. Tz'u-hsi began ruling the country in 1862, when her six-year-old son by Emperor Hsien-feng ascended to the throne. Then 27, she remained in power even after his death and the failure of the Boxer Rebellion, the 1900 anti-Western uprising she encouraged. Nor did Tz'u-hsi ever stop scheming. In 1908, from her sickbed, she ordered that the then emperor — her nephew — be poisoned. He died a day before she did.

TIME INC.

→

VICTORIA

In 1837, one month after her 18th birthday, she became Queen of the United Kingdom of Great Britain and Ireland. Hers was a prosperous kingdom thanks to the ongoing Industrial Revolution, which England had launched. Hers was also the greatest colonial empire of the 19th Century, which she expanded even farther. In 1876, she added Empress of India to her list of titles. She ruled for 63 years, the longest reign in English history, and rightly lent her name to an age.

TIME INC.

A FOOTBALL FIRST

On New Year's Day, 1902, 8,500 college football fans — some on horseback — watched the inaugural Rose Bowl in Pasadena, California. Every play on offense was a run; forward passes were illegal until 1906. And touchdowns and field goals both counted five points. Under any rules, it was a blowout: University of Michigan 49, Stanford 0.

BEATING THE ODDS

Though blind, deaf and mute before age two, Helen Keller (near right) was, by 22, enough of a celebrity to pose with famous actor Joseph Jefferson (far right) in 1902. She was then attending Radcliffe College, from which she graduated cum laude. Keller's real teacher was Anne Sullivan (center), the partially blind "miracle worker" only 14 years older than the pupil she had drawn into the world. Sullivan also interpreted for Keller at college and later accompanied her on world lecture tours to promote rights for the disabled. Keller wrote several books about her experiences.

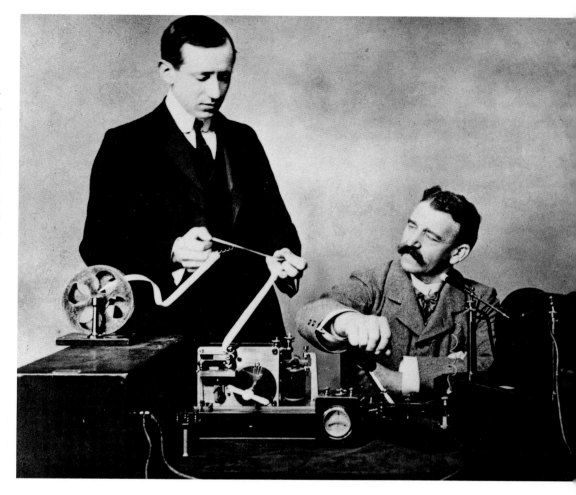

. . .

Dot-dot-dot (Morse code for the letter S) was the message the 27-year-old Guglielmo Marconi (near right) and aide G. S. Kemp received on December 12, 1901. The two had been in Newfoundland — and the code sent from Cornwall, England, 1,800 miles away. The Italian-Irish Marconi won the 1909 physics Nobel for his contributions to the infant medium of radio.

PIX INC.

SAY CHEESE . . .

What does *Kodak* stand for? Nothing. *Kodak* is the trade name invented by George Eastman in 1888 because he liked the letter *K*. The ex–bank clerk, then 26, went on to invent ever-better film and cameras. No Kodak product had more impact than his 1900 box Brownie, which fulfilled Eastman's wish to make "the camera as convenient as the pencil."

EASTMAN KODAK CO.

THE WRIGHT STUFF

Yes, the brothers Wright were inventors — but they were also businessmen. After all, it was in their bicycle shop in Dayton, Ohio, that Wilbur and Orville built their flying machines. They did have the foresight to position a photographer to document *Wright Flyer*'s first journey. But after extensively testing *Flyer No. 2* in the summer of 1904, they shunned the limelight to work out improvements — and to patent their designs. Not until 1908 did they go public by way of field trials for the U.S. Army (a $25,000 contract) and for the French (who paid them $100,000).

WE HAVE LIFTOFF!

After rolling down a 60-foot track, Orville Wright, 32, soared past Wilbur and into history. That first powered flight, on December 17, 1903, at Kill Devil Hills, North Carolina, ended after 12 seconds and spanned all of 120 feet. But the last of the day's four trials covered an impressive 852 feet.

TIME INC.

FATAL LANDING

Observers at the 1908 Army trials of the Wrights' two-man plane in Virginia hoisted the wreckage of the downed craft to free pilot Orville, who emerged with a broken leg, hip and ribs. The men at far right were tending to his passenger, who was not so fortunate; Lieutenant Thomas Selfridge died of head injuries, the first victim of the air age. Cause of the crash: One of the new extra-long wooden propellers split. Though the Wrights had made flights as long as 70 minutes, the Army was more interested in speed. To pass these trials, the plane had to average a dangerous 40 mph.

A City Is Shaken

Thirty-five years after Chicago was destroyed by fire, a 1906 earthquake totaled San Francisco. The main tremor on April 18 lasted less than a minute but was thought to have neared 8.3 on the Richter scale (invented in 1935, with a top value of 10). Worse was the blaze that began shortly after this photo was taken. When the last flames were put out three days later, as many as 3,000 people were dead or missing, and 225,000 — more than half the city's residents — were homeless.

NOAA / NESDIS

Art Takes a New Shape

Western painters were searching for new directions when a 26-year-old Spaniard named Pablo Picasso painted a radical, form-fracturing vision. His 1907 *Les Demoiselles d'Avignon* was the spark that ignited the art movement called Cubism. At first unsure of what he had created, Picasso didn't share the work with the public until 1916.

Museum of Modern Art

Uptown, Downtown

By 1902, New York City's 3.4 million citizens were no longer well served by the rickety, sunlight-blocking elevated transit lines that had begun sprouting in the late 1870s. The solution: Follow the example of London (1863), Budapest (1896), Boston (1897) and Paris (1900) by moving transportation underground. Manhattan's first subway opened in 1904 with a nickel fare. By 1940, there were 462 stations along a 230-mile route (93 miles of it aboveground) criss-crossing the entire city.

Lewis W. Hine / New York Public Library

HELLO, AUTOMOBILE!

In 1907, he hadn't solved where to put the spare tire (held by a worker at right); yet Henry Ford, 44, was proud to show Detroit the model for his new horseless buggy. The next year he put the Model T on sale for $825. By the time the Model T, also known as the Tin Lizzie, gave way to the Model A, in 1927, Ford had sold 15 million worldwide — and pioneered modern assembly-line production.

HENRY FORD MUSEUM

←

CHILDREN AT WORK

Her name is unknown, as is the age of this young cotton spinner from Newton, South Carolina. What is certain: In the 1900s, one-eighth of the South's textile workers were under age 12 (and most tobacco- and cotton-field workers under 10). Industries relying on child labor fended off reforms until 1938 — when unemployed Depression adults wanted those jobs.

LEWIS W. HINE / NEW YORK PUBLIC LIBRARY

NO WAY OUT ALIVE

Panicked seamstresses escaped burning alive by leaping 10 stories from a New York sweatshop in 1911; the Triangle Shirtwaist Company bolted its exits every day until quitting time in a cruel effort to get maximum production from its workers. Of 500 workers (mostly immigrant women aged 13 to 23), 146 died that day. Factory owners had to pay 23 families $75 each but were acquitted of manslaughter.

COURTESY OF ILGWU

←

CHILLING NEWS

A year after America's Robert Peary led the first party to success-fully reach the North Pole, a British team under Robert Scott sailed *Terra Nova* to Antarctica hoping to win the race to the South Pole. They reached it on January 18, 1912 — only to find a note left 35 days earlier by Norway's Roald Amundsen. Scott, 43, and his men starved to death on their return trip.

TIME INC.

THE PATH BETWEEN THE SEAS

Mariners had long dreamed of channeling through Colombia's narrow Isthmus of Panama to link the Atlantic and Pacific Oceans, thereby spar-ing themselves the 7,000-mile haul around South America's Cape Horn. In the 1800s, a French group began digging but ran out of money. In 1902, Teddy Roosevelt petitioned Bogotá to let a U.S. team try. Rejected, he encouraged a group of Colombians to form their own country — and then promptly accepted from this new Republic of Panama a sea-to-sea right-of-way that would be guaranteed forever. When TR went in 1906 to inspect the Big Ditch, he became the first sitting president to travel beyond America's borders. The 40-mile-long, 500-foot-wide, 40-foot-deep Panama Canal opened for traffic in 1914 after 10 years, saving ships thou-sands of miles and many days of travel; it cost $352 million and some 5,600 lives, mostly workers who fell victim to tropical diseases.

AP

NEW WORLD, NEW LIVES

These two tots had just emerged from the immigration hall at New York's Ellis Island, the last stop on their long journey to America. Between 1899 and 1907, immigration quadru-pled as the vibrant American economy demanded ever more workers. Most immigrants passed through Ellis Island because 90 percent of the newcomers sailed from Europe; racially inspired bans on Asians (primarily the Chinese) were lifted only in 1943. During its years of operation, 1892 to 1954, an estimated 12 million immigrants entered the country through Ellis Island.

AUGUSTUS FRANCIS SHERMAN / NEW YORK PUBLIC LIBRARY

"Iceberg Right Ahead!"

A contemporary British rendition of *Titanic*'s collision with an iceberg also showed the ship's immensity. The top seven of its decks were for passengers, the bottom four levels for machinery, provisions and cargo.

Time Inc.

Valor and Disgrace

When Macy's co-owner Isador Straus, 67, refused a lifeboat seat as the ship went down, so did his wife, Ida, 66. Not all first-class passengers were so brave. British aristocrat Sir Cosmo Duff-Gordon and his wife objected to rescuing survivors from the sea, though there was room for 28 more in their 40-person boat.

Courtesy of Straus Historical Society

Grave Secrets

The rust-draped prow, or front part of the ship, as well as the rest of *Titanic*'s exterior sit atop a muddy seabed. The Ballard team documented the wreck on videotape and in 53,000 film stills. Remote-operated cameras also snaked inside the superstructure to capture items like a bathtub, dishes and utensils, leather shoes, and a bottle of champagne, cork still intact.

Emory Kristof / NGS Image Collection

"Near, Far, Wherever You Are . . ."

Straddling the movie set prow, Leonardo DiCaprio, 23, and Kate Winslet, 22, stirred teenage hearts in 1997's *Titanic*. But their charisma alone could not account for the $1.8 billion worldwide gross of the century's No. 1 blockbuster movie. Director James Cameron, 43, descended in a Russian submersible (small underwater research craft) to film the wreck. More important, he wrote the romantic screenplay and oversaw the special effects, which humanized a night that will long be remembered.

PARAMOUNT PICTURES

From Triumph to Tragedy

Other shipwrecks have resulted in disastrous losses (the Mississippi side-wheeler *Sultana* burned in 1865, killing 1,500); yet it is the *Titanic* that haunts us. Why? Because we believed technology was infallible. One trade journal wrote that the *Titanic* was virtually unsinkable. The claim was echoed by its builders, its owners, its captain, even its awed passengers. Similar boasts have since issued from designers of bridges, zeppelins, space shuttles and PC software. All it took was one big piece of ice to prove everyone wrong.

MASTER OF THE SHIP

To mark Captain E. J. Smith's 43 years at sea, White Star gave its retiring top skipper a farewell gift: command of *Titanic*'s first crossing from Southampton, England, to New York. The ship left port April 10, 1912, and soon began picking up radioed warnings of icebergs ahead — including seven on April 14. Yet Smith, 62, never ordered the ship to slow down. He went down with the ship.

TIME INC.

Harriet Tubman
1821–1913

Born on a Maryland plantation into slavery, she fled north in 1849. Yet Tubman kept going home to help other blacks (among them, her parents) board the Underground Railroad. The "railroad" was a network of courageous people who helped slaves escape northward toward freedom. During the Civil War, Tubman posed as a servant in her native South in order to spy for the Union.

Florence Nightingale
1820–1910

She led 38 nurses to the Crimea on the Black Sea in 1854 to tend wounded troops, only to be cursed by British army doctors for her meddling. But the troops adored their "Lady of the Lamp" for making nightly rounds; she sailed home a hero. Nightingale founded the world's first school of nursing in 1860 and in 1907 became the first woman honored with Britain's Order of Merit.

Geronimo
1829–1909

Broken treaties forced his tribe of Chiricahua Apaches to a corner of Arizona with neither water nor game, so Geronimo led one of the West's last major Indian uprisings, finally surrendering in 1886. A rebel with a cause? Yes. But he was a guest of honor at Theodore Roosevelt's 1905 inauguration — and ended his days as a farmer in Oklahoma.

SUSAN B. ANTHONY
1820–1906

Angry that her teaching pay was one-fifth a male's, she protested by quitting and joining the temperance movement, which protested the sale and consumption of alcohol. Then, at 32, Anthony and fellow reformer Elizabeth Cady Stanton began to champion female suffrage, or the right to vote. U.S. women would not get to vote in a national election until 1920. But for her groundbreaking crusade Anthony was, in 1979, the first native-born woman to be commemorated on an American coin.

MARK TWAIN
1835–1910

In 1876, Mark Twain gave the country a charming young hero named Tom Sawyer. Eight years later he finished one of America's great novels, *Adventures of Huckleberry Finn*. Samuel Langhorne Clemens, who used the pen name Mark Twain, of Hannibal, Missouri, was blessed with an ear for language and a skeptic's eye. He used both to become a master storyteller.

TIME INC.

THE WAR TO END ALL WARS

1914–1919

Some 30,000 British troops had just arrived to defend Mons, a dreary Belgian mining town, when, on August 23, 1914, the Germans attacked, 160,000 strong. The British held their front — but not the large French force on their far right. Retreat was sounded. The Germans followed deep into France. Thoughts of a quick Allied triumph vanished. Between 1914 and 1919, 6.2 million Englishmen (out of an adult male population of 20.5 million) fought in the war. More than 744,000 did not return home.

TIME INC.

A NEW KIND OF WAR

by Jane Yolen

Ask any adult what happened between 1914 and 1919, and the answer will most likely be "the War to End All Wars." That war — which we now call World War I — began in 1914 and went on in Europe for some time before America finally got into it.

The spark that lit this particular fire was an assassin's bullet in Sarajevo on June 28. But it was a spark on dry kindling. Relations among the countries of Europe were already tense. When Archduke Ferdinand, heir to the Austro-Hungarian Empire, was murdered by a Serb nationalist, the flames erupted. They engulfed both Western and Eastern Europe, with Germany at the red-hot center of that conflagration.

For three years, America's president, Woodrow Wilson, kept the United States out of what seemed to be just another European battle and none of America's business. The news from the battlefronts was appalling. Young men in the millions were being slaughtered in the trench warfare. In Verdun in 1916, a five-month siege took the lives of 300,000 Germans and just as many Frenchmen. That same year, 420,000 British men and boys died along the Somme River. By war's end, in Russia alone the dead and wounded mounted into the millions.

What made this war so different was poison gas. The German generals had agreed on the use of mustard gas in 1915, and it took over a year before any country developed a reliable working mask to protect its soldiers. Ghastly yellow clouds of gas floated over the battle-grounds where the youth of Europe lay coughing and dying in the mud. Almost an entire generation of young European men was wiped out in the war.

The German government had also authorized submarine warfare, and ships bound for Britain and France became major targets. Some of those ships were American.

On April 2, 1917, President Wilson told a joint session of Congress, "American ships have been sunk, American lives taken."

Four days later, on a wave of patriotic fervor, America entered the war.

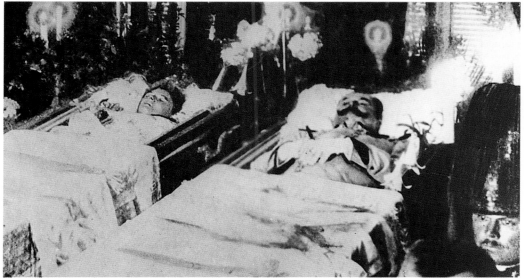

THE GREAT WAR BEGINS

Europe had enjoyed an uneasy peace for 44 years when on June 28, 1914, Archduke Franz Ferdinand, heir to the Austro-Hungarian Empire, left city hall in Sarajevo, provincial capital of Bosnia and Herzegovina, with his wife. Their car was just under way when Serbian nationalist Gavrilo Princip, 19, began shooting; Duchess Sophie was 46, the archduke 50. In less than 10 weeks, nine nations had assembled and launched the Great War.

TIME INC. (2)

One of the great problems President Wilson faced immediately was to expand America's fighting force. The relative strength of army to population in 1910 was the same as it had been in 1800. In March 1917 that force stood at only 190,000 men. By November 1918, it was 3,665,000 strong. Wilson gathered his doughboys — slang for American soldiers — by calling up the reserves, by appealing to the spirit of patriotic adventure in college boys, but mostly by conscripting (drafting) from the vast pool of illiterate, poor, black or immigrant populations.

But that pool of conscripts proved another sort of problem for President Wilson, because he had to get those varied immigrant communities to back the war effort somehow. Wilson feared where immigrant loyalties lay. At that time, one in every three Americans was either foreign-born or had at least one parent born outside of the United States.

Among the people the American leaders enlisted for help in the war effort were songwriters. As someone once

A DEADLY DEVELOPMENT

Two U.S. Signal Corpsmen were braced for a weapon new to World War I: poison gas. Though the 1899 Hague Convention banned chemical warfare, Germany began using gas in 1915. At first, Allied and German soldiers alike (the yellow clouds turned with the wind) had no protection beyond a wet hankie. It took a year to develop a working mask.

CULVER PICTURES

said, "A singing army is a cheerful army. A cheerful army is invincible."

Irving Berlin's popular soldier's complaint "Oh, How I Hate to Get Up in the Morning," George M. Cohan's jaunty "Over There," the ever perky "Pack Up Your Troubles in Your Old Kit Bag and Smile, Smile, Smile" by George Asaf, and other songs did as much for the war effort as anything else.

Song leaders were chosen in the military camps, and the sight of 10,000 young soldiers singing in unity was — so it was said — a sight that was both thrilling and astonishing.

Little palm-size books of songs were printed for the fighting men by the Commission on Training Camp Activities of the Army and Navy Departments, because as Major General Wood remarked, "It is just as essential that a soldier know how to sing as that he should carry rifles and know how to shoot them."

Salesmen for Liberty bonds were "gingered up" — meaning fired up — at daily meetings by song singing. The whole country seemed to be singing itself into a military fervor.

From the excitement, an outsider might be fooled into thinking the War to End All Wars was the only thing that happened between 1914 and 1919. But it was not.

American labor leader Joe Hill was executed by a firing squad in 1915 on trumped-up charges in the hopes of breaking the labor movement, which was an organized attempt by workers to improve their status by united action, especially via labor unions.

Early American feminist Margaret Sanger was arrested twice, in 1915 and 1916, for preaching about the importance of contraception (birth control).

On Easter Monday 1916, Irish nationalists seized key sites in Dublin and surrendered after a short battle with British troops, only to have 15 of their leaders executed.

In 1917 the Russian Revolution started when starving Russians began to riot in Petrograd. Tsar Nicholas abdicated his throne. Then he and his entire family were taken away to a rural estate in the Ural Mountains, where they were brutally murdered by the very soldiers sent to guard them. Eventually the Communists took over running Russia, a changeover that was to last almost the rest of the century.

In 1918 Spanish influenza killed half a million people in America and twenty million people worldwide. More died by flu than by guns, gas or starvation.

Still, it was the War to End All Wars that dominated the five years between 1914 and 1919, consuming not only millions of lives but the minds and hearts of the world leaders.

When the war ended, the League of Nations was set up, the organization that preceded the United Nations. The League had been President Wilson's pet project. He had hoped it would heal the wounds of war and make certain that peace would reign from then on. Alas, the U.S. Senate would not ratify the League's treaty, and Wilson, crippled by a stroke in October 1919, never regained his health.

Europe's health, too, was critical. Everyone had suffered, but Germany — the major loser in the war — suffered the most. Twenty years later, the Germans would try to regain what they had lost so ignobly. Ironically, the seeds of the even more brutal World War II were planted in the aftermath of the War to End All Wars.

Jane Yolen is the author of more than 200 books for children and young adults. Her book Owl Moon *won the prestigious Caldecott Medal, and* The Emperor and the Kite *was a Caldecott Honor title. Ms. Yolen has been awarded the Kerlan Award and Regina Award for her work. Other books include* The Devil's Arithmetic, *a National Jewish Book Award winner, and* The Seeing Stick, *winner of the Christopher Award.*

ST. PETERSBURG RULES

All was mercifully quiet on the eastern front for Russian officers guarding the Carpathians, the mountains between their motherland and Hungary. Manpower was not an issue — in 1914, after 125,000 Russians were captured by the Germans at Tannenberg, Czar Nicholas II just ordered more serfs drafted. But firepower was an issue — one-third of the Russian soldiers lacked guns. By the end of the war, Russia's dead, wounded or captured exceeded nine million troops.

TIME INC.

→

BOTCHED CHANCE

The goal: Land 75,000 British, Australian and New Zealand troops on Turkey's Mediterranean coast and drive up the Gallipoli Peninsula to Istanbul, the heart of the Ottoman Empire. The April 1915 invasion went well — but then Commonwealth leaders chose to slow their advance. The Turks rallied. By mid-May, 25,000 Allies were dead or wounded; by year's end, the surviving troops were evacuated.

TIME INC.

←

PLANNING PARENTHOOD

Twice in 1916 Margaret Sanger landed in New York courts for preaching contraception. First the ex-nurse, 36, was charged with obscenity for mailing pamphlets that described techniques; the case was dismissed. Later she served 30 days in the Queens County Penitentiary for opening, in Brooklyn, the nation's first clinic to advise on birth control (a term coined by Sanger).

CORBIS / BETTMANN-UPI

IRELAND DIVIDED IN TWO

On Easter Monday, 1916, Dublin's tranquillity was broken when Irish nationalists seized key sites to protest British rule. The British struck back, violently attacking the main post office and forcing a quick surrender. The British then executed 15 leaders of the uprising. That blunder aroused patriotism and led to the 1922 creation of the predominantly Catholic state now known as the Republic of Ireland.

TIME INC.

ACROSS THE RIO GRANDE

The last foreign troops to invade the Lower 48 were led by Mexico's Pancho Villa. After helping oust the dictators Porfirio Díaz and Victoriano Huerta, he fell out with fellow rebels. In 1916, Villa, 38, and his loyalists shot up Columbus, New Mexico. John Pershing and 4,000 U.S. soldiers chased him for a year across northern Mexico. They never caught him.

TIME INC.

THE RUSSIAN REVOLUTION BEGINS

In early 1917, the Russians were left with little food and fuel since all resources were going to the war effort. They began to riot, most notably in the newly renamed capital of Petrograd (later renamed Leningrad). Czar Nicholas had barely survived an uprising in 1905. Now he left the throne. A provisional government soon fell to the Reds (Communists), who were counterattacked by the Whites (the czar's loyalists). And so began the Russian Revolution.

TIME INC.

31

WEST SIDE STORY

From Romeo and Juliet to Tony and Maria? Composer Leonard Bernstein and choreographer Jerome Robbins originally planned a dance-driven update of Shakespeare's classic story set on New York's turn-of-the-century Lower East Side. But by 1957, the other side of town was hotter: Conflict between whites and Puerto Ricans had taken the place of Catholics versus Jews. Only in America . . .

HANK WALKER / LIFE

OKLAHOMA!

For a country beaten down by the Depression and then war, this first tuneful collaboration of Rodgers and Hammerstein, in 1943, was like a breath of fresh air. Based on the play *Green Grow the Lilacs,* it was the first musical to use choreography (by the ballet-trained dancer Agnes de Mille) to advance the story.

GJON MILI / LIFE

←

MY FAIR LADY

George Bernard Shaw's 1913 stage hit, *Pygmalion,* had stumped all attempts at musicalization until Frederick Loewe and Alan Jay Lerner took a shot. Their 1956 show — weaving together book and song — starred Rex Harrison and a young actress with a four-octave voice, Julie Andrews, 20.

LEONARD McCOMBE / LIFE

AIN'T MISBEHAVIN'

Sixty-five years after black musical revues were limited to being shown uptown in Harlem, Broadway decided that the most important color was green, the color of money. Richard Maltby Jr.'s groundbreaking 1978 tribute to the one-of-a-kind pianist-composer Fats Waller sparked a run of hits that mined black song and dance, among them *Jelly's Last Jam* and *Bring in da Noise, Bring in da Funk.*

MARTHA SWOPE / TIME INC.

←

RENT

Broadway was ruled by the British megahits of Andrew Lloyd Webber, such as *Phantom of the Opera,* and by expensive revivals when playwright Jonathan Larson arrived in 1996. His rock opera reset Puccini's 1896 opera *La Bohème* in New York's East Village to the tune of electric rock, Motown, reggae, salsa, even gospel. Modern social issues included AIDS, homelessness, and drug addiction. Three weeks before opening night, Larson died unexpectedly of heart failure caused by an aortic aneurysm; he was 35.

JOAN MARCUS

Enter Singing

In 1900, in an unruly part of Manhattan's West Side, theaters were being built to hold audiences of 1,500. Finally, the best acting talents had found a home on Broadway. Playwrights, musicians and lyricists came together to create a uniquely American art form, in which songs, and later dance, advanced the story — a formula copied worldwide. Soon rival mass entertainments emerged: Hollywood, radio, TV and broadcast sports. Today, Broadway's biggest theater still holds just 1,933. And while rumors of the death of Broadway have often circulated, none have turned out to be true.

SHOW BOAT

Based on Edna Ferber's 1926 best-selling novel, *Show Boat* was about entertainers traveling on a Mississippi paddle wheeler. Jerome Kern and lyricist Oscar Hammerstein II spent 14 months crafting from it a drama laced with complex social issues (such as interracial relationships) — a first on Broadway — and a score that, like "Ol' Man River," jus' keeps rollin' along.

Rogers and Hammerstein Organization

33

A MASSACRE — AND A MYSTERY

The impending turmoil seemed not to faze Nicholas (center, with heir apparent Prince Alexis, 14; his four daughters, ages 17 to 23; and palace guards). The imperial family soon surrendered to the Reds and was taken to an estate in the Ural Mountains in Russia to await a trial that was really to be a public display of the Reds' power. But on July 16, 1918, as the White Army neared, the czar and czarina, the five young Romanovs and four servants were slain with guns and bayonets. The 11 corpses were removed from the bullet-pocked room, doused with acid and tossed in an unmarked grave. Yet Soviet officials exhuming the remains in 1991 found only nine bodies.

TIME INC. (2)

THE YANKS ARE COMING

Private T. P. Laughlin of the New York National Guard said goodbye to his family in 1917 after being called to active duty. Reacting in part to German submarine attacks on U.S. merchant ships, America ended its neutrality despite having an army with fewer than 130,000 men. But the first doughboys (a slang term for troops since Custer's time) were in France by June and in combat by October.

NATIONAL ARCHIVES

OVER THERE, IN THE AIR

A former top race driver and world record holder for speed driving, 27-year-old American Eddie Rickenbacker earned his wings during the war. Before Armistice Day on November 11, 1918, he shot down 26 German aircraft. His competition was Manfred von Richthofen, known as the Red Baron because he painted his plane red. The Prussian Richthofen downed an average of one Allied plane per week (or as many as 80 in total) over France until he was finally shot down in 1918.

NATIONAL ARCHIVES

THANK YOU, MY FRIENDS

M. and Mme. Baloux of Breuilles-sur-Bar heartily thanked a couple of Yanks in 1918. Doughboys had helped liberate their village, occupied by Germans for four years. Battle casualties in France claimed the lives of 1.4 million native sons, as well as half the 112,500 Americans who died during the war.

INVISIBLE ENEMIES

Near war's end, two fevers swept America. Seattle cops wore masks in 1918 to guard against Spanish flu, a strain targeting those aged 20 to 40. Carried across oceans by returning soldiers, it killed half a million in the United States, 20 million worldwide. The societal virus — the Red Menace of Bolshevism — would take far longer to run its course.

→

"SAY IT AIN'T SO"

In 1919, Joe Jackson, 31, had another All-Star year (.35 average, 96 RBIs) to lead his White Sox to the World Series But when the underdog Cincinnati Reds won, he and seven teammates were charged with fixing the outcome o behalf of gamblers. Shoeless Joe said it wasn't so, and th jury agreed. But baseball banned him and the rest of th Chicago Black Sox for life. The innocence of America pastime was lost forever.

FREE AT LAST

Three-quarters of the 200,000 black sent overseas during World War I served as servants or musicians. Black women seeking to be nurses were flat-out rejected. But the 369th Infantry, here sailing back to New York in 1919, was different. The Harlem Hellfighters not only went toe-to-toe with the Germans but also became the first U.S. unit to reach the Rhine River.

RUSSIA TURNS RED

Here, Vladimir I. Lenin, a 49-year-old revolutionary, preached communism in Moscow's newly renamed Red Square. Just two years earlier, he had been forced to sneak back to Mother Russia inside a boxcar. In 1917, Czar Nicholas had left his throne — and in the following chaos, Lenin saw opportunity. Rightly so. By 1919, the civil war had been won, and his Bolsheviks were in power.

WAS THIS TRIP NECESSARY?

They rolled out the carpet for Woodrow Wilson in Dover, England, one month after the truce ending World War I. The president, 61, then sailed to peace talks in France. He would play a pivotal role in forging the Treaty of Versailles. Congress, blind to issues beyond America's borders, rejected not only the agreement but also U.S. membership in the newly proposed League of Nations, which laid the groundwork for the United Nations formed after World War II.

NATIONAL ARCHIVES

JOHN MUIR
1838–1914

When his family left Scotland for Wisconsin, young Muir was delighted to have a chance to explore America. The adult naturalist's articles about his wilderness treks spurred the federal government to carve out 13 national forests safe from commercial exploitation. Muir then roughed it in Yosemite National Park, located in the Sierra Nevada, with Teddy Roosevelt, who later created the federal parks system.

SIERRA CLUB

FRANK WOOLWORTH
1852–1919

Until he opened a store in Lancaster, Pennsylvania, in 1879, Woolworth had failed to make low-price retailing work. He soon turned his concept of pricing most items at five or ten cents into a Main Street staple; at its height, the Woolworth chain had 8,000 locations worldwide. Competition from discounters eventually destroyed the chain. Now the Venator Group, it sells sports gear.

BROWN BROTHERS

←

WILLIAM F. CODY
(BUFFALO BILL)
1846–1917

Buffalo Bill's exploits as an Army scout and buffalo hunter captivated novelists — but did Native Americans no good. Trading on his wild reputation, Buffalo Bill launched his Wild West show in 1883; it featured cowboys and Indians (including Sioux chief Sitting Bull) and even a cowgirl (Annie Oakley). Despite the barnstorming troupe's popularity, Cody died poor.

TIME INC.

PIERRE-AUGUSTE RENOIR
1841–1919

A teenage job decorating porcelains and fans led him to study art. Then, with Claude Monet, he put aside academic tradition and hauled his easel outdoors. (Their peer Frédéric Bazille executed this 1867 portrait.) Unlike his fellow Impressionists, Renoir preferred to paint figures. When arthritis crippled his hand, he had brushes tied to his arm so he could paint.

ERICH LESSING / ART RESOURCES

ANDREW CARNEGIE
1835–1919

The young Scot's first job in America: bobbin boy at a cotton mill. He reached management at the Pennsylvania Railroad but quit at 38 to found the firm that became Carnegie Steel. J. P. Morgan paid him $250 million for it in 1901; Carnegie devoted the rest of his life to giving away money, much of it to fund public libraries across the country.

REQUIEM

BOOKER T. WASHINGTON
1856–1915

Neither birth as a slave nor poverty dimmed his dreams. In 1881, in the belief that vocational skills were the fast track to racial equality, Washington founded a college, Tuskegee Normal and Industrial Institute. For his practicality and his friendships with influential whites, some rival black leaders deemed him an Uncle Tom, or a black who acts submissively toward whites.

1920–1929

Here she comes, the first Miss America. In 1921, fair maidens from nine cities traveled to Atlantic City to compete to be the first Miss America. The winner: Margaret Gorman, 16, of Washington, D.C. (second from left).

CULVER PICTURES

"GET HOT!"

by Avi

When I was a boy growing up in the 1940s, my parents rented out rooms in our house. One of the tenants was a philosophy professor who lived on the top floor. Aside from studying philosophy, he liked to brew beer. Fan my brow (Twenties slang for cool). How did a philosophy professor come to learn to make beer? It was something he learned during the time — in the Twenties — known as Prohibition, when it was illegal to purchase alcoholic beverages in bars or clubs.

Nothing quite captures the contradictory nature of America during the Twenties than the story of the 18th Amendment to our Constitution, which outlawed the commercial making and selling of liquor. On the day it went into effect, January 16, 1920, America went dry. But did it really?

With the ban in place, a number of things happened. The *legal* sale of liquor ceased. (Sales of soda pop went way up.) But the *illegal* making, smuggling and selling of drinking alcohol skyrocketed. Moreover, illegal drinking in clubs — called speakeasies — became common. Lots of people became "cellar smellers," those with a knack for finding places where liquor was being sold and served. Many, such as our philosophy professor, learned to make their own beer or spirits — like bathtub gin. In other words, Prohibition led to a kind of casual lawlessness that prevailed among all ranks of people, right up to and surrounding the presidency, such as Attorney General Harry Daugherty and Secretary of the Interior Albert Fall, who were implicated in the Teapot Dome scandal, which involved corruption and bribery. It was felt that as long as you didn't get caught, drinking and the bribery, corruption and other crimes that made it possible were okay. This culture of organized crime, gangs and violence was, in part, why people called the period the Roaring Twenties.

The words conjure up a period of good times for all, with prosperity from top to bottom. And nothing seems to represent the spirit of the times more than the "flapper." Here was a liberated young woman, presumably free of Victorian restraints and self-censorship, who asserted herself as an equal with men. In so doing, she claimed her right to have political views and to vote, as well as the right to smoke cigarettes and dance the Charleston in short skirts wherever she so chose. The term "sex appeal" was coined. Beauty parlors bloomed. (But equal pay for equal work — if the young woman could even get the work — was still another matter.)

But personal lives did change. It was discovered in the 1920 census that for the first time more people in the U.S. lived in cities than in rural areas. Car ownership became common. Mass advertising came into its own. You could pay for things on the installment plan. Radio, with increasingly numerous stations, could be heard all over the country. Movies — first silent, then with sound — became more of an American passion than ever before, creating such stars as Clara Bow (the "It" girl), Douglas Fairbanks, Laurel and Hardy, Mickey Mouse. Sports figures emerged with national, as contrasted to regional, recognition: people such as the champion boxer Jack Dempsey and New York Yankee Babe Ruth, who set a home-

PROHIBITION BEGINS

America went dry on January 16, 1920, as the 18th Amendment, banning alcohol, kicked in. Revenuers hunted for stashes; flappers hunted for speakeasies where liquor was secretly being poured. Before Prohibition's repeal 13 years later, many illicit bootlegging fortunes would be made.

CULVER PICTURES

run record of 60 in 1925. Women athletes were recognized on their own terms, too, with such individuals as Gertrude Ederle, the English Channel swimmer.

Then there was Charles Lindbergh, whose solo airplane flight across the Atlantic in 1927 seemed to combine — in one dashing young man — the ideals of technology and the pluck of handsome youth.

But while some of the decade's positive and boisterous reputation is well deserved, a good deal is not. The United States, almost alone among the World War I combatants, had emerged with its land mass untouched and — compared with European countries — relatively few casualties. Economically its strength was unrivaled. Nor had its political system been really challenged.

Nonetheless, the European revolutions, particularly the Communist takeover of the Russian Revolution, frightened many business and industrial leaders, as well as government legal officials, who had a great deal of power. A Red Scare replaced feelings of security. While many Americans artists flocked to France, many other Americans succumbed to notions of insularity, developing strong opinions about what was good

JAZZ GENIUS

One-of-a-kind Louis Armstrong (center, with King Oliver's Creole band in 1922) was a trumpeter extraordinaire whose solo improvisations were the bridge from blues and ragtime to swing and beyond. Satchmo, as he was nicknamed, also invented scat when he dropped the sheet music during a recording session and ad-libbed nonsense syllables.

PHOTOGRAPHER UNKNOWN

One-tenth of one percent of those at the top received as much income as 42 percent of those at the bottom combined. Thousands upon thousands died because of bad working conditions. Even more were disabled for life. Great numbers lived in poor conditions. As the decade progressed, rural workers and farmers increasingly struggled to survive. Pennsylvania steelworkers worked 12 hours a day, six days a week. No wonder workers — even policemen — joined unions in great numbers. By joining unions, the individual worker gained bargaining clout with the strength of numbers. What these people wanted was higher salaries, better working conditions. But unions were labeled as un-American by the establishment and were suppressed, often violently.

While this was the period that women were finally given the right to vote in federal elections, political diversity was discouraged. For this, too, was the time when the Ku Klux Klan came back into being as a violent organization opposed to Afro-Americans, Catholics, Jews and immigrants. The KKK, as it was called, with more than 4.5 million members, virtually dominated some areas as well as whole states, such as Indiana. Vicious racism, organized or personal, was rampant as well as deadly.

Simultaneously, this was a period when the arts truly flourished. Jazz began to be widely appreciated as a unique American contribution to music. Photography, architecture, dance, as well as

for America, labeling contrasting views as "un-American." The fact is, many Americans who wished to buy into the American Dream, that is, to better themselves and their families, were accused of un-Americanism. What was "un-American"? Socialism. Greater freedom for women. Support for unions. Being opposed to racism. Not believing that business was the most important aspect of America.

This was not a trivial matter. If you were deemed un-American, you could be harassed, deported, jailed, even killed. Without doubt, workingpeople's wages went up each year for most of the decade. Still, the economic profile of America was lopsided. Debt greatly increased.

literature developed unique American voices. In the face of widespread censorship of some European writers, distinct American fiction by such authors as Willa Cather, F. Scott Fitzgerald and Ernest Hemingway took hold.

And let's not overlook the fact that the Twenties were also the decade that saw the acceptance of books for children as a special literary field. Book publishing created children's book departments, and the creation of the Newbery Medal in 1922 lent dignity and recognition to the world of children's books.

A Channel Crossing

Two years after winning a gold and a pair of bronzes at the 1924 Paris Olympics, Manhattan-born Gertrude Ederle, 19, became the sixth person — and first woman — to swim the English Channel. Her time for the grueling 35 miles was the fastest yet by nearly two hours. But Ederle's 14½-hour effort aggravated an ear problem that later left her deaf.

Culver Pictures

In short, the Twenties were full of contradictions. It was a time of fun, wealth and freedom for some; despair, poverty, restrictions for others. "Get hot!" was a Twenties slang expression meaning "come alive!" The trouble was, things got *too* hot, exploded and died. It was as if, after all, the roar of the Roaring Twenties was a lot of bunk. For on October 29, 1929, the stock market crashed, plunging the nation into the Great Depression, which lasted more than a decade.

Avi is the author of two Newbery Honor books, The True Confessions of Charlotte Doyle *and* Nothing but the Truth. Poppy *won the* Horn Book *award for best fiction.* Encounter at Easton *was a Christopher Award winner, and* The Fighting Ground *won a Scott O'Dell Award for Historical Fiction. He has also won numerous state children's choice awards.*

←

FALSELY ACCUSED?

In 1920, shoemaker Nicola Sacco, 29 (right), and fish peddler Bartolomeo Vanzetti, 32, were charged with a double murder and robbery in South Braintree, Massachusetts. Despite flimsy eyewitness testimony and Sacco's confirmed alibi, the Italian-born anarchists were convicted. All requests for a retrial were denied — even after a local hood confessed to the crime in 1925. Their executions, in 1927, sparked worldwide protests.

CORBIS / BETTMANN-UPI

MEET KING TUT

In 1923, workers in Egypt removed artifacts from an obscure pharaoh's tomb that had been sealed since 1323 B.C. Inside, British archaeologist Howard Carter, 50 (inspecting the royal coffin), found a stash of funerary art far more significant than Tutankhamen himself. (The king had been murdered while still a teenager.)

METROPOLITAN MUSEUM OF ART

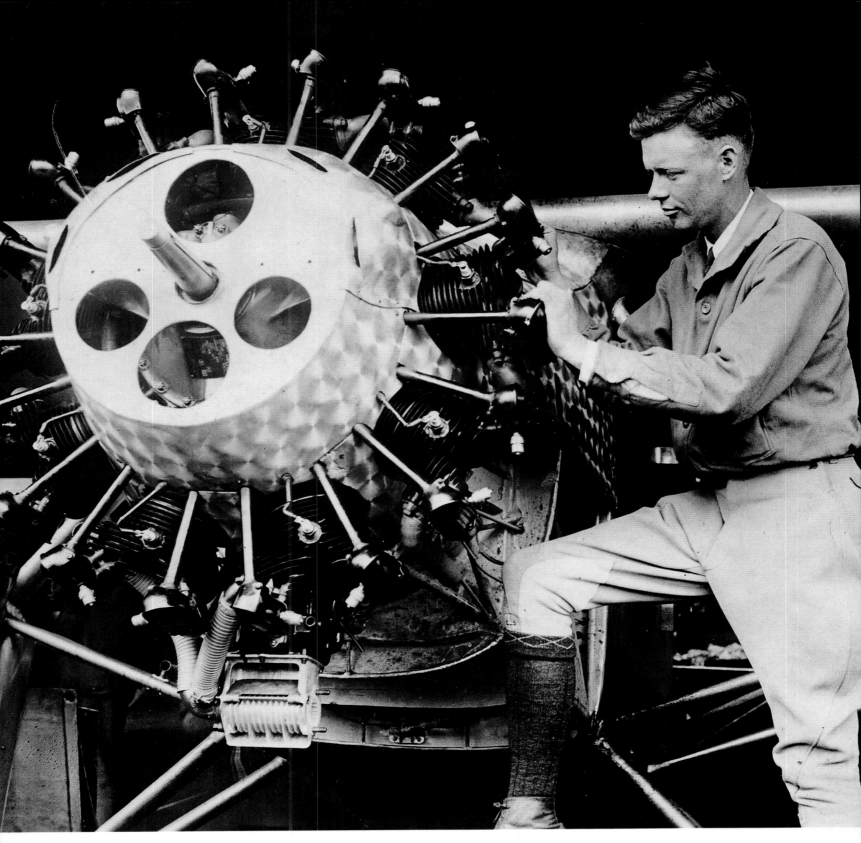

LUCKY LINDY

The prize for the first nonstop flight from New York to Paris: $25,000. On May 21, 1927, airmail pilot Charles Lindbergh, 25, not only claimed the money by flying the 3,610 miles in 33½ hours but also became a worldwide hero for doing it solo. After hopping over to England in *Spirit of St. Louis,* where thousands cheered, he returned to America. By ship.

PUBLIC NUISANCES

New York mayor George B. McClellan was no doubt unavailable when suffragettes called on City Hall in 1908; police officers made sure the ladies didn't linger. Things were better out West. Wyoming entered the Union in 1890 with the first constitution to grant women the vote in state and local elections.

CULVER PICTURES

PEACE IN HER TIME

The first U.S. congresswoman (representing her native Montana) could vote for herself in 1916 but not for a presidential candidate. Jeannette Rankin lost her next run after opposing America's entry into World War I. Her continued pacifism, opposition to war (above, in 1932, at age 51), led to a second term in 1940; she thereupon became the lone legislator to vote against declaring war on Japan after Pearl Harbor.

AP

A PIONEER APPOINTEE

The 1933 Senate confirmation of Frances Perkins, 51, as Secretary of Labor made her the first female cabinet member. Though neither industry nor labor thought she was very tough, she helped craft New Deal laws on unemployment compensation, minimum wage, maximum workweek and Social Security. Perkins resigned in 1945, two months after the death of her mentor, FDR.

AP

You Go, Girl!

The Founding Fathers didn't specifically exclude the Founding Mothers from a role in democracy, they just never considered it. Things began to change with the opening of the American West, where gender counted for less than can-do spirit. By the late 19th Century, many states had rewritten laws allowing women to own property. Yet calls by suffragettes, women campaigning for voting rights, were met with amusement; in 1900, women could cast ballots in a national election only in New Zealand. In 1918 the U.S. House of Representatives supported a woman's right to vote, but Southern senators balked at giving black women this right. Congress finally passed the 19th Amendment the following year. By the end of the century, women had achieved every major elected and appointed post in the country except the two highest: president and vice-president.

HERE'S TO WINNING THE VOTE

On August 18, 1920, after Tennessee had become the 36th state required to ratify the 19th Amendment into law, Alice Paul lifted a glass (of grape juice, not alcohol, thanks to the 18th Amendment). Paul, 35, later worked to make sure gender-equality passages were included in the United Nations charter and the U.S. Civil Rights Act of 1964.

WELCOME TO "THE CLUB"

Triumphant four-term representative Margaret Chase Smith, 52, of Maine won the GOP nomination for the Senate in 1948. When she went on to win the election, she became the first woman to sit in both houses of Congress. Smith, whom Eisenhower considered for vice-president in 1952 before choosing Richard Nixon, served four terms in the Senate.

"UNBOUGHT AND UNBOSSED"

This was the slogan of Brooklyn's Shirley Chisholm, who in 1968, at 43, became the first black congresswoman. She proved just as feisty on the Hill. Named to a sub-committee overseeing forestry, Chisholm asked aloud if that was because House leaders knew little about Brooklyn, which has no forests. They caved. She won reelection six times.

HERE COMES THE JUDGE

Fifty-one-year-old Sandra Day O'Connor was the surprise nominee of Ronald Reagan to become the 102nd justice of the Supreme Court. In 1981, the Arizona jurist became the first woman confirmed to the High Court. Twelve years later, O'Connor was joined by Ruth Bader Ginsburg.

DAVID HUME KENNERLY

RAINDROPS KEPT FALLING

An autumn shower in 1984 didn't dampen the spirits of Geraldine Ferraro, the first woman major-party candidate for vice-president, and Democratic ticket head Walter Mondale, 56. The ex-congresswoman, 49, held her own in a televised debate. But Election Day turned stormy: The opposing Republican duo, Reagan-Bush, captured even Ferraro's home state of New York.

DIANA WALKER / TIME

CUTTIN' LOOSE

It looked goofy (even when performed by Tempest Stevens and Swedish pole vault champ Charles Hoff at a 1926 contest in Los Angeles), but hey, giddy times spawned jazzy fads. In fact, the Charleston sprang from traditional dances of West Africa and Trinidad as transformed by Southern blacks. And it survived the Roaring Twenties: Charleston-inspired rock steps, such as the Hully Gully, the Watusi and the Mashed Potato, were to follow.

CORBIS / BETTMANN-UPI

DARWIN ON TRIAL

At 65, his three runs for the U.S. presidency long past, William Jennings Bryan agreed in 1925 to help the state of Tennessee prosecute John T. Scopes, 24, for teaching evolution. Opposing counsel Clarence Darrow called on Bryan to defend the Bible's version of creation. He could not. Still, Scopes was found guilty (a verdict later overturned). Five days after the verdict, Bryan died of a heart attack.

REACHING SKYWARD

More than financial stocks were soaring in Manhattan. When work got under way on the 1,048-foot Chrysler Building in 1928, a rival business group quickly hatched plans to raze the original Waldorf-Astoria Hotel and put up a 1,250-foot skyscraper (right), the Empire State Building.

BEFORE THE MOUSE

In 1926, animator Walt Disney, 25 (third from left), posed with his entire staff and Margie Gay, the star of his *Alice in Cartoonland* series. At the time, Disney's studio was rodentless — and struggling. Two years later, however, along came *Steamboat Willie* and a mouse named Mickey (whose pipsqueak voice was provided by Walt himself). Among other accomplishments, Disney went on to create the first full-length cartoon movie, *Snow White and the Seven Dwarfs,* and to win 26 Academy Awards.

LET THE GAMES BEGIN

When his pay hit $80,000, baseball legend George Herman Ruth was asked why he deserved a salary larger than President Hoover's. Cracked the Babe, or so it was reported, "I'm having a better year." Before World War I, the most widely known and rewarded athletes were boxers, whose prizefights were described in every newspaper. Then came radio and the need to fill hour upon hour of empty airtimes. Sporting events were cheap to broadcast. An America with abundant leisure time and pocket cash responded, transforming mere diversion into an industry. The Twenties were a time for heroes to emerge and profit. Some, like Babe Ruth, did.

GOING, GOING, GONE . . .

The Baby Ruth candy bar was in fact named for President Cleveland's infant daughter. The New York Yankee slugger Babe Ruth played hard and lived harder. The Sultan of Swat is best known for hitting 60 home runs in the 1927 season and 714 home runs in his 21-year career. Babe Ruth helped baseball escape the long shadow of its 1919 Black Sox scandal.

CORBIS / BETTMANN-UPI

SWIMMING TO TINSELTOWN

Romanian-born, Chicago-reared Johnny Weissmuller quit ninth grade to focus on swimming. In addition to setting 67 world marks, he won three Olympic golds in 1924 and another pair in 1928. Weissmuller then went Hollywood, playing Tarzan 12 times before ending his acting career as big- and small-screen hero Jungle Jim.

JANZTEN, INC.

→

FORE!

It wasn't his exquisite game that made Bobby Jones an idol, nor his run of 13 major titles in eight years. Instead, it was the wonder of an amateur (and full-time lawyer) repeatedly besting the top pros. After winning the Grand Slam in 1930, Jones, 28, withdrew from competitive golf to help found and nurture the Masters tournament in his native Georgia.

HUTLON DEUTSCH / LIAISON

WYATT EARP
1848–1929

An authorized biography cemented his reputation as a fearless lawman. But many in Tombstone, Arizona, wanted to hang its deputy marshal and his pal Doc Holliday for slaughtering members of the Clanton Gang at 1881's O.K. Corral shoot-out. The next year, accused of murdering two men suspected of killing his brother Morgan, Earp escaped farther west.

KANSAS STATE HISTORICAL SOCIETY

LIZZIE BORDEN
1860–1927

They never found the ax with which she allegedly gave her mother 40 whacks (and, went the chant, her dad 41), so the jury acquitted the 33-year-old Sunday school teacher of the 1892 homicides. Though the target of critical whispers, Borden never moved from her native Fall River, Massachusetts.

FALL RIVER HISTORICAL SOCIETY

ANNIE OAKLEY
1860–1926

As a young girl in Ohio, the future trick-shot artist got her gun and hunted small game to help pay the family mortgage. Next Oakley set her sights on larger prey: noted marksman Frank Butler, whom she outshot in a match and then married. When the high-caliber couple joined Buffalo Bill's Wild West show, the Peerless Lady Wing-Shot got top billing. It was rumored that she could shoot a playing card full of holes from a distance of 90 feet.

PHOTOGRAPHER UNKNOWN

REQUIEM

ENRICO CARUSO
1873–1921

Music lessons were out of reach for a poor Neapolitan with 19 siblings. He made up for lost time. At 21, with only three years of training, Caruso debuted in his hometown. Soon the tenor's extraordinary voice and dramatic delivery won worldwide acclaim. But a ravenous appetite for food and tobacco shortened the career — and life — of opera's biggest star.

FRANK LERNER

ALEXANDER GRAHAM BELL
1847–1922

Teaching speech to the hearing impaired led Bell to experiment with the electric transmission of sound. While the telephone, which he invented in 1876 at age 29, could not help his favorite deaf pupil, Mabel Hubbard, she married him anyway. Bell also devised a kite to carry people and bred sheep more likely to bear twins.

TIME INC.

EMPTY POCKETS

1930–1939

On a summer day less than 10 months after the Great Stock Market Crash of 1929, 6,000 out-of-work New Yorkers lined up at a state employment agency; 135 lucky ones found jobs. It would soon get worse. By 1932, almost 30 percent of America's labor force was looking for work.

YEARS OF HILARITY AND HEARTBREAK

by Robert Cormier

When I remember the Thirties and the Great Depression and the drumbeats of war coming from Europe, I think of my father sitting beside the old Emerson radio in the kitchen, listening to the voices of doom and disaster on the six o'clock news. Later, the comic voices of Amos 'n' Andy always caused him to chuckle a bit. On certain evenings, the ringing voice of President Franklin Delano Roosevelt during one of his "fireside chats" softened the harsh worry lines on his face. "We have nothing to fear but fear itself," FDR said at his inauguration in 1933. My father took hope from those words even though the factory where he had labored for 22 years at the comb-making machines could now give him only part-time work.

I also remember the Saturday movie matinees at the Plymouth Theater downtown, where my friends and I endured the newsreels while waiting for the double features to start — the "B" movie with the exploits of Charlie Chan or Sherlock Holmes followed by the "feature presentation" starring James Cagney or Joan Crawford. We viewed the newsreels — "The Eyes and Ears of the World" — impatiently, not realizing that we were absorbing those stark black-and-white images of world and national events into our subconscious while waiting for the westerns and mysteries and romances to fill that magic screen.

The radio and the movies were the great influences of a Thirties childhood, introducing my friends and me to the reality and fantasy of that troubled era.

We were linked to our world by images: We could not pass a house with a leaning ladder without shuddering at the thought of the Lindbergh baby snatched from his bedroom by a kidnapper, and we could not watch the newsreel armies of Adolf Hitler goose-stepping through the streets of Germany without thinking of soldiers, stationed at nearby Fort Devens, who walked our downtown streets on weekends. In his novel *The Grapes of Wrath,* John Steinbeck chronicled the desperate flight of the Joad family from the dust bowls of Oklahoma to the

DIMPLED DYNAMO

Before Shirley Temple turned eight, she was earning $2,500 per week for singing, dancing and charming in such hit movies as *Little Miss Marker* and *The Little Colonel*. Unlike many child stars before and since, Temple's life had a solid second act: a good marriage and public service that included two years as U.S. ambassador to Ghana.

CULVER PICTURES

We knew, however, that the vacation was not all that it seemed to be. In the wake of layoffs and short time in the factories, fiery and disgruntled workers sought to unionize the shops, to gain some control over their jobs and their lives. Strikes were threatened and strikes were called. Some factory owners took steps to avoid unionization by voluntarily providing sudden benefits for workers. That's why my father basked in the knowledge of being paid for not working that week, ignoring for the moment the seasonal layoff that was sure to happen in August.

green promise of California, but here in my hometown of Leominster, Massachusetts, scores of men, my father among them, had gone from factory to factory and finally to distant cities in their own desperate search for work.

I remember the steaming summer of 1937 when my father and I strolled down Fifth Street on a Tuesday afternoon, my father marvelling at the fact that he was actually earning money for "doing nothing," his first paid one-week vacation.

Hilarity and heartbreak were the disparate twins of that turbulent era. On that magic Plymouth movie screen, we laughed at the merry absurdities of the Marx Brothers and felt the ache in our throats as fading sunlight foretold Bette Davis's death in *Dark Victory*. In the outside reality of Pleasant Street in our hometown, we saw people lined up at the "commissary" for the weekly grocery order from the government in a program called relief, a dreaded word and prospect for my father and one of the reasons he persisted in job searches during layoffs at the shop.

But real life was not all grim in the Thirties, not at the age of 12 or 13 or 14. We had our heroes, and some of them were less than legitimate. Gentleman John Dillinger robbed banks

DEAD AIM ON CRIME

The criminologist in J. Edgar Hoover led him to modernize the FBI, which he took over in 1924, at age 29. The spin doctor in him invented the Public Enemy (usually some gangster his agents were set to nab). Hoover swore until the 1960s that there was no organized crime in America, yet kept his job through eight presidencies, until his death in 1972.

TIME INC.

the frenzied first round of their bout. What made this victory all the sweeter was the fact that Schmeling had defeated Louis in their first encounter, which seemed symbolic then of Hitler's blazing conquests in Europe. We wondered, as we sat stunned at the radio, whether Hitler would someday aim his armies and his guns at us, here in the United States. But, ah, that second battle brought sweet revenge and somehow made us feel invulnerable and not fated for defeat. In the Olympic Games of 1936, Jesse Owens, the U.S. athlete, dashed and leaped to victory against Hitler's vaunted Aryan (white, Christian) "supermen" as the frustrated dictator watched. In a dark-

LEAPING INTO HISTORY

By winning a record four events at the 1936 Berlin Olympics, Jesse Owens, 22, foiled Adolf Hitler's dream of showcasing Aryan superiority. Ironically, he qualified for the long jump only after a tip from Luz Long of Germany. Owens went on to take gold, Long the silver. The two stayed in touch until Long was killed in Italy during World War II.

POPPERFOTO / ARCHIVE

with utter politeness, and we mourned a bit when he was betrayed in movielike fashion by a woman in red. We marveled at the Robin Hood exploits of "Pretty Boy" Floyd, who shared his robbery loot with those less fortunate. But we also rooted, without realizing the irony, for J. Edgar Hoover and the FBI agents who tracked down those gun-wielding "public enemies."

Two of our real-life heroes acted as our surrogate challengers to Adolf Hitler, doing what we could not do, accomplishing what we could not accomplish. Joe Louis, the black heavyweight champion of the world, brought Hitler's white boxing warrior, Max Schmeling, to his knees in

Nothing but Dust

To farm folk fleeing the Dust Bowl engulfing the Southwest, anything beat what they had left behind — even makeshift quarters on the road west. The most popular destination of these internal immigrants: California.

AP / Wide World

ened theater half a world away, we cheered our Olympic champ.

The third decade of the 20th Century, in the grimness of the Depression, with overtures of war filling the air and our fathers still uncertain about jobs and work, may appear to have been a dark, hopeless time in our lives. But hope arrived at decade's end at the 1939 New York World's Fair. There, along with millions of others, we saw so many marvels of the coming age on dazzling display, symbolized by a magical device called television, which plucked pictures from the air and flung them on a screen, providing us with a glimpse into "the world of tomorrow," the fair's bright theme with all its promises.

We did not know whether those promises would be kept or what the new decade would present to us. But we were young and brave and hopeful, and eager to step into that beckoning world.

Robert Cormier is an award-winning journalist and has written more than 15 young adult novels, including the Lewis Carroll Shelf Award winner The Chocolate War *and* I Am the Cheese, *both of which were made into major motion pictures. He was awarded the Margaret A. Edwards Award honoring his lifetime achievement in writing for teens, and some of his other books include* Heroes, Tenderness, Fade *and* After the First Death.

Look Away, Look Away

In 1931, Alabama cops caught 11 people stealing away on a freight train. Two were white women who claimed that the others, black youths aged 13 to 20, had raped them. Doctors found no evidence; yet eight of the "Scottsboro Boys" (named after the town where they went on trial) were convicted and sentenced to die. The Supreme Court ruled against Alabama twice before the state gave up. Still, Clarence Norris (second from left) remained in prison until 1946.

A League of Her Own

America's woman athlete of her time (perhaps of all time) took the gold in the javelin and the hurdles at the 1932 L.A. Olympics and lost the high jump only because the judges didn't like her unconventional style. Babe Didrickson also starred in hoops and baseball before focusing on golf in 1934. She won 50-plus titles, including a third U.S. Women's Open at 40 despite recent cancer surgery. Babe died 26 months later, in 1956.

THE WINNING TICKET

Two-time New York governor Franklin D. Roosevelt, 50 (left, with running mate John Nance Garner, 63), was the 1932 Democratic candidate for the White House. In public, he used leg braces to hide the effects of the disease polio. His campaign speech on his whistle-stop tour (as in Goodland, Kansas, below) promised "a new deal" and Prohibition's repeal. FDR's victory was a landslide. He went on to be elected to a record four terms as President.

CORBIS / BETTMANN-ACME

INSET: AP

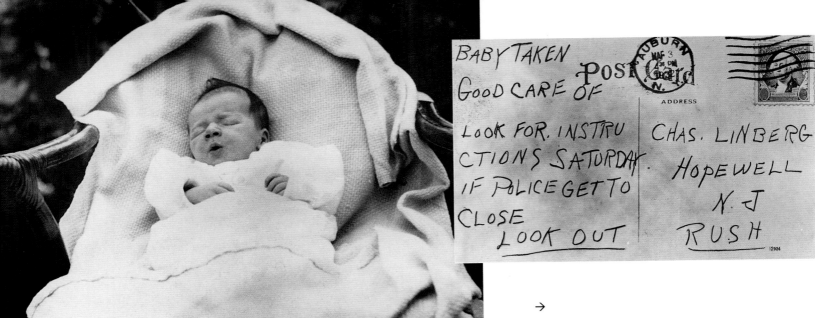

WANTED: BABY KIDNAPPERS

Charles Lindbergh Jr. was 20 months old when he was taken from a second-floor bedroom of his hero father's rural New Jersey mansion on March 1, 1932. The nation was transfixed. Clues abounded (a ransom note, a ladder), as did cruel hoaxes (above right). On April 8, the Lindberghs paid $50,000 in marked bills for a fruitless tip. On May 12, their son's body was found just five miles from home. Three years passed before a German-born carpenter spent part of the $50,000. Bruno Hauptmann was electrocuted in 1936.

ABOVE: CORBIS / BETTMANN

ABOVE RIGHT: AP

→

RAISE A GLASS!

After 14 years, booze was finally legal again! One Clevelander (lower right) couldn't wait! Prohibition was repealed in 1933 after Utah, of all states, ratified the 21st Amendment, negating the 18th Amendment, which had banned the manufacture and sale of alcohol. It wasn't until 1970 that America tried more social engineering, when Congress outlawed marijuana.

NEW YORK TIMES / ARCHIVE PHOTOS

IN NEED OF A NEW DEAL

Rural America was especially devastated by the Great Depression. In 1935, a federal relief worker visited a threadbare Tennessee family to determine its need for help. From 1933 to 1941, FDR's domestic-aid programs channeled billions of dollars to those in need.

CARL MYDANS / FSA

GRAPES OF WRATH

A bad drought in the 1930s teamed with bad farming practices turned 150,000 square miles of the Great Plains into the Dust Bowl. In New Mexico and four other states, families packed up their belongings and caravanned west. By decade's end, California's population had grown by 22 percent.

LIBRARY OF CONGRESS

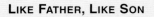

LIKE FATHER, LIKE SON

At 45, John Gotti vaulted atop New York's Gambino crime family by having capo Paul Castellano whacked. The publicity-loving "Dapper Don" smirked at Feds until a pal ratted. In 1999, serving life, Gotti, 58, learned that the heir to his mob, son John Jr., 35, was joining him behind bars.

BILL SWERSEY / GAMMA LIAISON

YOUNG, CRIMINAL, AND IN LOVE

In 1934, Bonnie Parker was 23 and her prisoner of love, Clyde Barrow, was 25. The Dust Bowl couple robbed banks, gas stations, etc. — 13 in 21 months. The law soon sprang a deadly ambush near Gibsland, Louisiana, as deadly as in the 1968 movie *Bonnie and Clyde,* starring Warren Beatty and Faye Dunaway.

CORBIS / BETTMANN-UPI

WHO ARE THESE GUYS?

Robert Parker, 34 (seated, far right), went by Butch Cassidy. Harry Longbaugh, 30 (seated, near left), went by Sundance Kid. Their Wyoming-based Hole in the Wall gang of robbers and rustlers was also called the Wild Bunch (but that's another movie). Butch and Sundance did flee to Bolivia in 1901. But where did they die? Butch near Spokane in 1937, claim some, and Sundance in Casper, Wyoming, circa 1957.

WESTERN HISTORY COLLECTION / UNIVERSITY OF OKLAHOMA LIBRARY

Beloved Badmen

A society is shaped by its laws but often defined by its outlaws. Americans bristle against authority, be it King George III or a speed-limit sign, so it is not surprising that we have long admired a certain breed of cocky crook. The criminal spirit of the James Gang and Billy the Kid, featured in the dime novels of the 1800s, didn't die with the Old West; it rode into the new century alongside Butch and Sundance. An outlaw jaunty enough to stop while on the lam to pose for a portrait? Why, that's the stuff of folklore, not to mention Hollywood, which has paid tribute to almost all these felons on film.

HE FOUGHT THE LAW — AND THE LAW WON

As a kid in Brooklyn, Al Capone practiced crime. He perfected it in Chicago, a city thrown wide open by Prohibition. The cops couldn't nail him for the cunning massacre of rival bootleggers on St. Valentine's Day, 1929. But two years later the Feds sent him to the slammer as a tax cheat. Capone died horribly of the sexually transmitted disease syphilis in Miami at age 48.

CORBIS / BETTMANN-ACME

PREACHING TO THE CHOIR

In 1934, accompanied by a group of Black Shirts, or Fascist supporters, Benito Mussolini, 51, worked a crowd in Venice using characteristic dramatic poses and fiery speech-making. The ex-Socialist had reshaped Italy in the 12 years since becoming its youngest prime minister. Unions no longer struck, trains ran on time. Mussolini also wanted to restore Rome's imperial grandeur, so in 1935, he invaded Ethiopia. Later, he allied Italy with Hitler's Germany.

ALFRED EISENSTAEDT / LIFE

ELIMINATING THE COMPETITION

Many of Joseph Stalin's evil deeds in the Thirties went unreported in the USSR. After Lenin's death in 1924, Stalin made a series of strategic political moves that eliminated much of the competition and put him in sole control of the USSR by 1930. After he collectivized farms, the ensuing famine may have killed 10 million. In 1934, with Leon Trotsky banished, Stalin had his last rival, Sergey Kirov, murdered. Still ahead: the Great Purge of 1936–1938, which claimed up to 10 million more.

PHOTOGRAPHER UNKNOWN

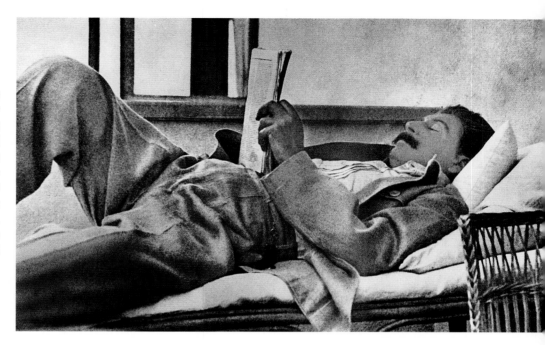

THE GREAT ESCAPE

In 1935, Mao Tse-tung, 41 (near left), and Chou En-lai, 37, had reason to be proud. A year earlier, facing military defeat by the government, they had retreated north with 100,000 guerrillas. After 6,000 miles, 24 rivers and 18 mountain ranges, 8,000 reached safety in Yenan. In 1949, Mao's Communists won control of China; Long March veterans retained power until 1997.

LATTIMORE FOUNDATION / COURTESY OF PEABODY MUSEUM

FLIGHT INTO TERROR

The *Hindenburg*, the pride of the German zeppelin fleet, was a rigid airship that relied on highly flammable hydrogen for lift. Only 76 feet shorter than the *Titanic*, it was billed as "the lightest hotel in the world" and was designed to carry passengers on 52-hour transatlantic flights. It was docking at Lakehurst, New Jersey, in 1937 when fire broke out. Miraculously, 61 of the 97 aboard survived.

WARD-BALDWIN / CORBIS / BETTMANN

A Hard New Regime in Spain

Three years after his assignment to a remote post in the Canary Islands for being a troublemaker, General Francisco Franco, 46, stood in Madrid as head of state. The price of power: a brutal civil war. In 1936, Franco, backed by Italy and Germany, led army units that helped right-wing Nationalists oust a shaky liberal government. The leftists, with Soviet aid, fought back. Franco's forces had more weapons. As *caudillo* — leader — he ruled Spain until his death in 1975.

DEVER

The Future Dalai Lama

A four-year search ended in 1937 when monks identified Bstan-'dzin-rgya-mtsho, age two, as Tibet's next spiritual ruler. In 1940, the boy was installed as Dalai Lama (the 14th since 1391). He was 15 when China overran his kingdom. The Dalai Lama escaped into exile in 1959; in 1989, he won the Nobel Peace Prize for his gentle campaign to win freedom for his homeland.

A. T. STEELE

Read All About It

Having fled to Mexico City to escape a wrathful ex-comrade named Joseph Stalin, Soviet theorist Leon Trotsky, 58, and his wife, Natalia, reviewed their plight in a new weekly magazine titled *Life*. His sin was to compete with Stalin for power after Lenin's death. Mexico proved not far enough from Russia: In 1940, a Soviet agent sent by Moscow assassinated Trotsky with an ice pick.

FRANCIS MILLER / LIFE

Labor Pains

"The chief business of the American people is business," said Calvin Coolidge in 1925. Left out of the equation: blue-collar workers, whose efforts to organize were often bloodily suppressed (Haymarket Square, Pullman, Ludlow). Management was still using hired thugs to bust strikes (Harlan County, River Rouge) when FDR's New Deal leveled the playing field. Collective bargaining — the process that allows wages, hours and working conditions to be negotiated by a union with an employer — was enacted in 1935, a minimum wage in 1938. What organized labor did not — could not — anticipate was America's evolution into a service economy in which the workers' collars were white.

Doing It the Hard Way

Violence was common at strikes in the Thirties. At a Pennsylvania steel mill, picketers learned firsthand that the man trying to cross their line, the Reverend H. L. Queen, was literally a management mouthpiece.

Corbis / Bettmann-Acme

Organization Men

When General Motors fired five men for wearing pro-labor buttons, co-unionists in Flint, Michigan, refused to leave their plant. They launched the first large-scale peaceful sit-down strike on December 30, 1936. They came prepared to stay — a union band entertained the strikers. After 44 days, GM gave in by recognizing the United Auto Workers union.

Corbis / Bettmann-Underwood

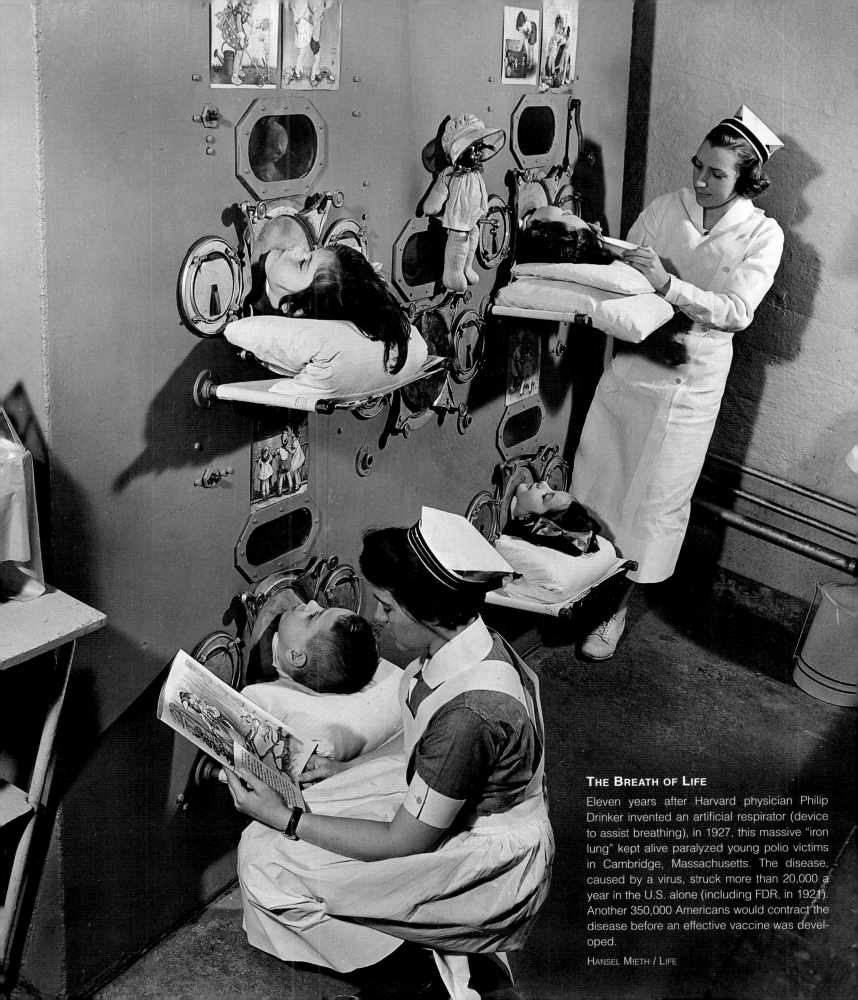

THE BREATH OF LIFE

Eleven years after Harvard physician Philip Drinker invented an artificial respirator (device to assist breathing), in 1927, this massive "iron lung" kept alive paralyzed young polio victims in Cambridge, Massachusetts. The disease, caused by a virus, struck more than 20,000 a year in the U.S. alone (including FDR, in 1921). Another 350,000 Americans would contract the disease before an effective vaccine was developed.

HANSEL MIETH / LIFE

The Greatest Year in Hollywood Ever—1939

The Thirties failed to depress the motion picture industry, which averaged more than 13 new movie releases every week of the decade. Sure, the stars moaned about being treated like property by the studios. Yet they were paid royally (James Cagney, $12,500 per week; Bette Davis, $4,000 per week) in an era when a steelworker earned $1,720 per year. And in 1939, the first generation of American moviemakers seemed to come of age at once. Never before, and never since, has Hollywood produced such a magical crop of entertaining, intelligent and enduring features in one calendar year.

WUTHERING HEIGHTS

Author Emily Brontë's wild moors were in Yorkshire, England. For budgetary reasons, though, Laurence Olivier, 32, and Merle Oberon, 28, filmed their movie scenes on the "moor" closer to Hollywood — they planted part of the San Fernando Valley with heather.

MOVIE STILL ARCHIVES

THE WIZARD OF OZ

Judy Garland showed her spunk at 16 by playing a 12-year-old from Kansas. Each day her breasts had to be painfully taped flat. But she and co-stars (from left) Bert Lahr, Jack Haley and Ray Bolger ended up smiling down the Yellow Brick Road to showbiz immortality.

MOVIE STILL ARCHIVES

GONE WITH THE WIND

It ate up 10 writers, three directors, a cast of almost 2,500 and a budget that today would equal $48 million. Yet the 220-minute (intermission not included) Civil War epic, based on the best-selling and Pulitzer Prize–winning novel by Margaret Mitchell, turned out to be engrossingly intimate, thanks mostly to the star power of Vivien Leigh, 26, and Clark Gable, 38.

MGM

←

MR. SMITH GOES TO WASHINGTON

Thirty-one-year-old James Stewart's aw-shucks decency was perfect for his role as a new senator standing up to special interests. Director Frank Capra went to Washington to show off his movie to the Capitol Hill crowd. Reviews were not kind, but Stewart was at the beginning of a long and lustrous film career.

COLUMBIA PICTURES

TOMORROW, THE WORLD

In 1938, Germany's Nazi Party staged its ninth late-summer rally in Nuremberg. The faithful had good reason to Heil their Führer. At 49, Adolf Hitler, the nation's chancellor and president since 1934, had just annexed Austria without a single shot being fired. Next up: Czechoslovakia, and then Poland.

HUGO JAEGER / LIFE (2)

EVIL BEDFELLOWS

Joseph Stalin (standing at right) and Nazi diplomat Joachim von Ribbentrop (standing in middle) traded smiles in Moscow on August 23, 1939, while Soviet foreign minister V. M. Molotov signed a nonaggression pact promising that the USSR and Germany would not to go to war with each other. The pact between the two archrivals stunned the world. Nine days later, the German army rolled into western Poland. On September 3, Ribbentrop honored a secret treaty and invited the USSR to breach Poland from the east; Stalin didn't have to be asked twice. The Soviet-German agreement would last 22 months, until Hitler changed his mind.

DEVER

AMELIA EARHART
1897–1937

In 1928, she was the first woman to fly the Atlantic — as a passenger. Four years later she repeated the trip — as the pilot. Earhart was also the first of either gender to solo from Hawaii to California, but her 1937 attempt to circumnavigate the globe fell short somewhere over the Pacific.

TIME INC.

JOHN D. ROCKEFELLER
1839–1937

He owned Standard Oil, a refining monopoly for 30 years before the Supreme Court broke it up in 1911. This made Rockefeller (here with John Jr.) not only one of the world's richest men but also a magnet for the era's photographers of celebrities (far left). After 1897, the billionaire spent his time on philanthropy, chasing young women and image-buffing (he dispensed new dimes to children).

CORBIS / BETTMANN-UPI

 ←

THOMAS ALVA EDISON
1847–1931

Deafness made him a misfit at school, so he educated himself. The boy began conducting chemistry experiments at 10 and never really left the lab. Over the next 74 years, Edison won an unprecedented 1,093 patents. Among his inventions: the record player, the incandescent lightbulb, a gizmo that became the ticker tape and the motion-picture camera.

NATIONAL PARK SERVICE

GEORGE GERSHWIN
1898–1937

Borrowing freely from both popular and classical music, America's most versatile composer developed an unrivaled musical vocabulary. Gershwin wrote symphonically *(Rhapsody in Blue)*, then crossed over to Broadway, collaborating with lyricist brother Ira on 1924's *Lady, Be Good!* and 10 other shows. Two years after writing his folk opera, *Porgy and Bess,* though, he was dead of a brain tumor.

EDWARD T. STEICHEN

REQUIEM

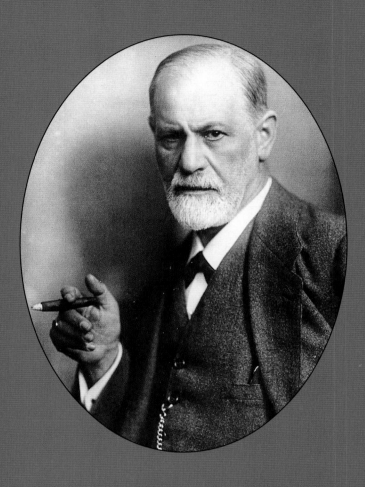

←

JAMES NAISMITH
1861–1939

The game of hoops he devised in 1891 at a YMCA college in Springfield, Massachusetts, was meant to amuse kids between football and baseball seasons. The first peach baskets went up with bottoms intact; someone had to fetch the ball after each goal. Naismith, who set them 10 feet off the floor, would no doubt be astonished by how much of today's basketball is played above the rim.

CORBIS / BETTMANN-UPI

SIGMUND FREUD
1856–1939

Sometimes a cigar is just a cigar; but thanks to the Austrian neurologist, we'll always wonder. Freud altered our understanding of behavior with his revolutionary theory that most human actions stem from unconscious desires. One of his most famous books was *The Interpretation of Dreams* (published in 1900), in which he analyzed many of his own dreams. The father of psychoanalysis could have used some counseling himself. His smoking habit led to an agonizing death from mouth cancer.

TIME INC.

1940–1945

Chungking, China's temporary capital, fell under savage Japanese bombing in July 1941. Japan had begun nibbling at China a decade earlier; it was time for the main course.

CARL MYDANS / LIFE

THE HOME FRONT

by Lois Lowry

In 1940 my parents took me to the New York World's Fair, which was by then in its second year. A clown shook hands with me. I rode on a carousel. A giant typewriter was exactly like the one my father had at home, but grown to the size of a house. On the Futurama ride, a train took us across an entire United States of the future, from coast to coast, in minutes. The world seemed bright-colored and splendid, filled with promise.

Perhaps adults, who read newspapers, knew that things were ominous and becoming frightening. But our world, that of childhood, was just as hope-filled and magical as the world we saw at the fair. We thrived on comic strips like *Blondie* and *Dick Tracy*, the square-jawed detective who relentlessly battled crime; movies (we weren't allowed to see *Gone With the Wind* because it was considered much too grown-up; but *The Wizard of Oz* had been released, and it captivated our attention instead); and games: we counted our way endlessly around the Monopoly board, gobbling up railroads, paying taxes and collecting $200 every time we passed GO.

The radio, a large piece of furniture in everyone's living room, was an ongoing part of our existence. We children sprawled on the floor and listened to George Burns and Gracie Allen and a show called *The Aldrich Family* that always opened with a mother's shout — "Hen-reeee! Henry Aldrich!" — and her adolescent son's squeaky-voiced reply, which we loved to mimic: "Coming, Mother!"

It almost seemed to be the radio that changed everything on a Sunday afternoon in late 1941. We didn't know what Pearl Harbor was, but we could see the horror on our parents' faces that day.

When our big brothers and young uncles and sometimes our fathers were ordered to report for duty and were issued armed forces uniforms, our mothers began to stitch heavy dark fabric into something called "blackout curtains" that were drawn across our windows at night.

Air-raid wardens prowling the neighborhood knocked on the door if they could see light and warned us that enemy aircraft would spot us from the sky.

Very soon we knew what the enemy would look like up close. Movies told us. The Germans were crew-cut and had glinting, evil eyes. *"Achtung!"* they said in guttural, threatening voices. The Japanese — we learned to call them "Japs" — had buck teeth, carried slashing bayonets and shouted, *"Banzai!"*

In some parts of our country, Japanese-Americans, thousands of them, lost their homes

FIRST LADY REDEFINED

Glamorous? No. Happily wed? No. But Eleanor Roosevelt (with GIs, short for "government issue," on the White House lawn in 1942) was smart and caring. She fought fearlessly for the have-nots until her death in 1962, at 78, and, in so doing, redefined the role of First Lady.

CORBIS / BETTMANN-ACME

and businesses and were taken away to internment camps. They didn't look like the enemy we saw in movies. They looked like our schoolmates and neighbors. They looked puzzled and stunned as they were led away.

DO WITH LESS — SO THEY'LL HAVE ENOUGH! a poster said, showing us a helmeted soldier, lifting

his tin cup and looking grateful that he had something to sip. So we did with less. Ration stamps were issued, limiting our meat, cheese and sugar. Butter disappeared, and we spread lard, tinted yellow with dye, on our toast. Three gallons of gas a week for cars — no more unless you were a doctor. Even our shoes: three pairs a year. Not really a hardship, unless you were growing fast! We created Victory gardens in our yards, dutifully planting seeds and canning our homegrown produce so that the boys in uniform would have enough.

And our moms gave up their silk stockings. Silk, after all, had come from Japan, now our enemy. Women painted their legs dark with special leg paint, fake stockings. (Dogs could tell, though. They always sniffed the paint.)

We removed the paper labels from store-bought canned goods, squashed the tin cans flat when they were empty, and carried them in bundles to school, where we donated them to the scrap drive, along with balls of tinfoil saved from gum wrappers. Somehow, we were told, these bits of metal would be manufactured into planes and tanks.

With our weekly allowance we bought fan magazines and read about the movie stars we liked best. Betty Grable, with her long bare legs, was a favorite pin-up girl of the GIs, we knew; and so was bosomy Jane Russell. The magazines told us how patriotic the actresses all were, doing volunteer work, serving coffee to soldiers, dancing with them before they shipped out. The jitterbug was what they danced. We tried it ourselves, playing fragile 78 rpm records on our big Victrolas and dancing in our living rooms. "Bell-bottom trousers, coat of navy blue / I love a sailor boy and he loves me too . . . ," we sang, even though we were

93

THE RACE CARD

For being born in the USA of Japanese ancestry, this child had to report, in April 1942, to a depot in California. In the wake of Pearl Harbor, a nervous nation forgot that there were far fewer Japanese-Americans than German- or Italian-Americans. Some 120,000 citizens of Japanese ancestry were shipped to barbed-wired camps in places like Minidoka, North Dakota. In 1989, Congress voted each surviving internee a reparation payment of $20,000.

DOROTHEA LANGE / NATIONAL ARCHIVES

too young for sailor boys and had to settle for the gawky Boy Scouts who lived in our neighborhood.

Life magazine was bringing news and pictures of the war to most American homes. *The Saturday Evening Post* was delivered once a week, and we liked the frequent Norman Rockwell covers best of all. He reproduced our own lives with their innocence and patriotism. In 1943, he introduced, on a magazine cover, a woman he called "Rosie the Riveter"; she represented so many of America's women — working now, for the first time, taking the place of the many men who had gone to war.

Some of them, we knew, would not come back. The newspapers had headlines of battles taking place far away, and we learned the names of islands in the Pacific: Corregidor, Guam, Saipan, Iwo Jima and Okinawa. Newsreels preceding the Saturday afternoon matinees showed pictures our mothers didn't want us to see: planes crashing into carriers, lifeboats filled with frightened sailors, bombed-out neighborhoods in London, people searching rubble for bodies.

Families hung emblems in their windows: small gold-fringed flags with stars. We children felt respectful when we saw the little flags, and sad when the stars on them were gold. Each blue star represented a family member in the service. A gold star was for a family member killed. "Gold star mothers" had lost a son; some lost more than one.

In 1942, a family named Sullivan lost all five of their boys when the light cruiser USS *Juneau* was torpedoed.

Even as we cruised the neighborhood on our bicycles (and woe to the child with a damaged bike tire! New ones were impossible to get) admiring Victory gardens and counting the little window flags, we were constantly on the alert for spies. Posters told us that they were out there, even in our quiet towns. People with foreign accents fell under our suspicion, and we wondered whether they were transmitting secret information to Hitler by hidden radio. We were vigilant children, prepared to warn the authorities if we discovered clues or evidence.

Many thousands of German, Italian and Japanese prisoners of war were housed in internment camps in the United States. One was not far from the small Pennsylvania town where I lived, and one summer evening an escaped German prisoner was caught in the yard next to mine as he tried to steal clothing that had been left on a clothesline overnight.

But for the most part, our lives were free of horrors. We played jump rope and hopscotch — even the neighborhood boys joined in sometimes. But when they played baseball, girls only watched. Girls played jacks. We drank Coca-Cola from pale green glass bottles. It was rumored that if you took an aspirin with a Coke, you would become drunk. I never knew anyone who dared try it.

When Franklin Roosevelt died suddenly in the spring of 1945, the moment felt the same as the day Pearl Harbor was bombed. Shock. People sat near their radios, listening. Mothers cried.

We didn't know our new president. Roosevelt had been part of our lives for years, and we could name his children and felt acquainted with his little dog. The man named Truman was a stranger to us, and we were suspicious of his ordinariness.

Yet it was he, Harry Truman, who told us that the war had ended. First, V-E Day (victory in Europe) in May, and we saw newsreels of the hordes of cheering people: strangers kissing one another and soldiers throwing their hats into the air.

Then, in August, victory in Japan. The news that the Japanese had surrendered was shadowed by the news of the bomb that had brought about their surrender. It was something so new, so immense, so terrifying that we didn't know what to think. What was an atom, anyway? What did *atomic bomb* mean? Who ever heard of a place called Hiroshima?

The mushroom-shaped cloud that we saw in the newsreels was someplace very far away. Our own skies were blue and uncontaminated. Our fathers and uncles would now be coming home. We would get new shoes, new cars, and we could turn the Victory garden back into a place for the swing set. The future was coming, and it would be free of war. It would be like the Futurama train at the World's Fair: unshadowed, sleek and safe. That's what we thought, when we were young, in 1945.

Lois Lowry has written more than 20 young adult novels, including two Newbery Medal winners, The Giver *and* Number the Stars, *which also won both the Dorothy Canfield Fisher and National Jewish Book Awards. She is the author of the popular Anastasia Krupnik series, as well as* A Summer to Die, *and the Golden Kite Award winner* Robbie Starkey *and the upcoming* Gathering Blue.

THE RUSSIANS ARE COMING

Finnish civilians took to the woods in early 1940 to wait out another Soviet air raid. Stalin, despite his nonaggression pact with Hitler, remained deeply suspicious of Germany's intent and sought to protect his northern border with a chunk of Finland. That nation of 3.8 million resisted with surprising ferocity; it held off the Red Army for more than three months.

CARL MYDANS / LIFE

BRITAIN BOMBED

Hopeless retreat ended Britain's first attempt to repel Hitler. In mid-1940, 200,000 British troops, plus 140,000 French and Belgian allies, were cornered in the Channel port of Dunkirk. The Brits assembled a 1,000-vessel fleet (ranging from warships to fishing boats) that, protected by the Royal Air Force, repeatedly made the 100-mile crossing. Over 10 days, all but 2,000 men were evacuated. A month later, Germany began air strikes on military sites in England in preparation for a cross-Channel assault. A retaliatory British bombing of Berlin so enraged Hitler that he ordered his Luftwaffe, the German air force, to destroy London. Not only was the Blitz beaten back by the vastly outmanned Royal Air Force, but the 40,000 civilian lives it claimed also stiffened British will. Hitler shelved the invasion set for September 15, 1940.

WILLIAM VANDIVERT / LIFE

VICTORY LAP IN FRANCE

Six weeks too late to enjoy April (1940) in Paris, German soldiers paraded past the Arc de Triomphe. In 32 days, they did what their World War I countrymen could not do in four years: occupy the French capital. To avoid the Maginot Line — a 200-mile French defense on its border with Germany — they had swept through the Low Countries of Belgium, the Netherlands and Luxembourg, displacing thousands.

HEINRICH HOFFMAN / LIFE

SPRINGTIME FOR HITLER

The early Forties were the best years of his wretched life. Since 1933, Adolf Hitler had pieced together an empire to rival ancient Rome's with little loss of German life. Starstruck socialites, awed Austrian schoolgirls and enchanted Nazi wives all worshipped from afar. However, Hitler lived with Eva Braun (here, at his Berchtesgaden chalet) from 1932 on. He would finally end 56 years of bachelorhood by marrying her on April 29, 1945, their next-to-last day on earth.

PHOTOGRAPHER UNKNOWN

ALL DEALS WERE OFF

On June 22, 1941, Adolf Hitler ignored his nonaggression pact with Stalin and sent 3.2 million Axis troops into the Soviet Union. Stalin quickly rejoined the Allies. Though Germany had better weapons, the USSR fought back with more men and Mother Nature (the bitter Russian winter came early that year).

AP / WIDE WORLD

→

A RUDE AWAKENING

On Sunday, December 7, 1941, at 7:55 A.M., sailors at the Pearl Harbor base in Honolulu, Hawaii, awoke to an infamous day. A Japanese fleet assembled by Harvard-educated Admiral Isoroku Yamamoto, 57, had crossed the West Pacific undetected. For two hours, 360 carrier-based attack planes pummeled Pearl. The U.S. lost 2,344 men, four battleships (14 other warships sustained major damage) and 200 fighter planes. Reason for the sneak strike: An American embargo of oil and steel was pinching the resource-poor nation's industries. It took Congress only 27 hours to declare war on Japan.

BALDWIN H. WARD / CORBIS / BETTMANN

Combat Overview— 1942–1944

1942: Japan, after victories at Pearl Harbor and in Malaya and Siam, was strengthening its control of Southeast Asia and the South Pacific. Its Axis partners ruled Western Europe by force or by collaboration (France, Norway) and had the upper hand in North Africa, thanks to German panzer general Erwin Rommel. And Hitler's Wehrmacht troops had survived their first Russian winter.

1943: The U.S. was advancing west in the Pacific. In Europe, the Germans were busy in the USSR and quelling resistance in other occupied lands. But there soon came a breakthrough. An Anglo-American offensive launched in late 1942 seized North Africa. The Allies quickly hopped across the Mediterranean and invaded Sicily. Hitler now had to fight a war on two fronts.

1944: In the Pacific, the Allies were taking back Japan's island conquests one by one. In Europe, Germany was exposed both to the east, where it had been repelled by the Soviet Union, and to the south, where Italy was easily overtaken by invading Americans. It was time for the Allies to make their big move.

A Cruel Sunrise on Bataan

By 1942, the Imperial Japanese troops had conquered the Philippines in five months. Surrendering at Bataan: 12,000 GIs and 64,000 Filipino soldiers. The Japanese forced their weakened captives on a 65-mile trek. Some 10,000 escaped on the way, but 5,600 did not survive the brutal Death March. Another 17,000 died in POW (prisoner of war) camps.

Tsuguichi Koyangi

VICTORY AT SEA

Naval warfare took on a new dimension in 1942 with two epic slugfests between the U.S. and Japan. Rather than exchange traditional attacks, the foes sent torpedo bombers (left) and fighters after each other's far-off warships. (By incredible luck, America's three Pearl Harbor–based aircraft carriers were at sea on December 7, 1941.) The fleets fought to a four-day standoff in May on the Coral Sea; then, on June 4, they met again off an island in the Central Pacific wanted by Japan as a base from which to menace Hawaii. The Battle of Midway began well for the U.S. as its planes sank three enemy carriers. That day, though, the flattop *Yorktown* was hit. Two days later, a Japanese submarine finished the job. American planes then sank a fourth carrier and the cruiser *Mikuma*. The Japanese, who also lost 332 planes, retreated west. The Pacific was America's.

FRANK SCHERSCHEL / LIFE

SLOW ROAD TO TOKYO

Two months after the Battle of Midway, 10,000 Marines landed on Guadalcanal. The Japanese-held island in the Pacific was astride a key sea-lane between the U.S. and ally Australia, then fighting to hold the island of New Guinea. Before withdrawing, Japan absorbed 23,000 deaths. America won its first offensive of the war — and got a taste of the difficulties of island combat.

RALPH MORSE / LIFE

THE BIG CHILL

Deep inside Mother Russia, German officers in standard-issue greatcoats surrendered to winter-camouflaged Soviet troops. Like Napoleon 130 years before him, Hitler saw his army falter because of overstretched supply lines and unsuitable clothing and weapons. (German rifles jammed in the cold.) Yet he refused to call off the invasion.

TIME INC.

THE END WAS NEAR

A late-1941 Nazi edict required all Jews, like this Berlin couple, to wear yellow Stars of David in public. This was only the latest edict targeting Germany's "undesirables." Jews, captured Slavs and others in the occupied countries were already being singled out for slaughter. Now Hitler impatiently demanded a "final solution." At a January meeting in Wannsee, high aides proposed using non-Aryans (people who were not Caucasian or Christian) as slave laborers. Camps were built. And some were fitted with "showers" that sprayed the deadly gas Zyklon B.

AP

No Place Was Out of Harm's Way

Bathing beauties may have seemed uppermost in the minds of U.S. airmen defending the Aleutian Islands, but this was serious business. The war's only ground action on American soil was fought on this string of islands in the Northern Pacific. In mid-1942, Japan landed troops on two islands; a year later, GIs evicted them. Peace reigned again. One Yank found time to write a third novel. His name: Walter Farley. His book: *The Black Stallion Returns*.

DMITRI KESSEL / LIFE

An Eye for an Eye

GIs paid dearly for their January 1943 amphibious landing on the island of New Guinea (here, one of the first photos of U.S. war dead to be cleared by government censors). So did Japanese defenders who had rushed down to the beach near Buna to press the fight. The Yanks were able to repel a Japanese advance on Port Moresby, a base on the island's south coast vital to the defense of Australia.

GEORGE STROCK / LIFE

THE FIRST DESERT STORM

In January, Allied captors herded 19,000 Italian and 6,000 German POWs to the Libyan port of Tobruk (in the distance). The westward pursuit of Germany's crack Afrika Korps ended, in May, at Tunis. North Africa was now clear of the Axis.

BRITISH WAR OFFICE

JUNE 6, 1944

Under General Dwight D. Eisenhower, 54 (right, on June 5), the Allies patiently arranged in England the largest invasion force in history. The target: the Normandy coast of France. On D-Day (the randomly chosen *D* had no significance), 5,000 airplanes and ships carried 175,000 men across the English Channel. The landings came under withering German fire.

LEFT: ROBERT CAPA / MAGNUM

RIGHT: U.S. SIGNAL CORPS

HITLER BETS THE FARM

By 1944, German buzz bombs, or self-guided missiles, had begun hitting London. And in December, Hitler mustered a massive ground strike on the Ardennes, woodlands that sprawl across France, Belgium and Luxembourg. The GI defenders, denied air support by bad weather, were at a serious disadvantage. U.S. armor proved no match for the enemy's new Tiger tanks. Rather than concede the Battle of the Bulge, the U.S. inserted airborne divisions that helped blunt the attack until skies cleared on Christmas Eve and Allied planes regained the air. America's toll: 20,000 dead, 40,000 injured, 20,000 captured. The Germans fared worse. Hitler was now facing the final moment of truth.

GEORGE SILK / LIFE

PRELUDE TO SLAUGHTER

In early 1945, five Marines and a Navy medic were captured on film raising the Stars and Stripes on the island of Iwo Jima. This memorable image of the Pacific conflict raised the morale of war-weary Americans at home. But because Iwo sat within easy flying range of Japan's Home Islands, it was defended by 23,000 troops. The Imperial troops fought on for another month, until only 216 were alive to surrender. Of the 30,000-plus Americans who waded ashore, 21,000 were wounded and 6,800 killed. Among the dead: three of the flag raisers.

JOE ROSENTHAL / AP

THE TICKET WAS ONE-WAY

Desperate to stem the tide, Japan in late 1944 began fitting fighter planes with 550-pound bombs; pilots were to plow the planes into U.S. warships. The maneuver was called *kamikaze*, or divine wind, after a typhoon that repelled an invading Mongol fleet in 1274. Though the suicide flights sank or damaged some 300 ships, including the carrier *Belleau Woods*, most were shot down short of their target.

EDWARD STEICHEN / U.S. NAVY

He Kept His Word

In January 1945, almost three years after Douglas MacArthur, his wife and their son had been ordered to evacuate the Philippines ahead of the approaching Japanese, the general, 64, strolled back through the surf at Lingayen Gulf. He was fulfilling his pledge, "I shall return." MacArthur brought 68,000 U.S. troops. In July, he pronounced the islands liberated.

Carl Mydans / Life

The Next War Begins

February 1945: To Yalta, a Crimean resort, traveled Winston Churchill, 70 (far left); Franklin D. Roosevelt, 63; and host Joseph Stalin, 65. With no other Allied leaders present, they devised a strategy to checkmate the Axis and drew up a postwar map. Stalin came away with rights to Eastern Europe. The seeds of the Cold War were sown.

National Archives / U.S. Army

When Words Fail

Some 11 million labor camp inmates died in the 100-plus compounds set up by the Third Reich in Germany and its captive countries. Allied leaders had known of a 1942 Nazi order to rid Europe of non-Aryans. Not until Germany's defeat, though, was the magnitude of Hitler's "final solution" apparent. The Allies rescued these gaunt inmates of Buchenwald, but the Holocaust claimed two-thirds of Europe's nine million Jews, as well as Slavs, Gypsies and homosexuals. Many families lost three generations. Coming to grips with guilt — among survivors, butchers, bystanders alike — would require more than the next three generations.

Margaret Bourke-White / Life

→

Halfway to Peace

From New York — where a replica Lady Liberty greeted the masses gathering in Times Square — to Los Angeles, America partied on May 7, 1945, as word spread of Germany's surrender. It came 68 months and 50 million deaths after Hitler invaded Poland. But V-E (Victory in Europe) Day jubilation was tempered; in the Pacific, there was a war yet to be won.

Tony Linck / Life

AUGUST 6, 1945

The silvery speck in the morning sky over Hiroshima, Japan, raised no alarms. What havoc could a lone U.S. B-29 wreak? From *Enola Gay*'s belly fell a single 9,000-pound bomb that detonated 2,000 feet above ground zero. The force of its fission-generated, 5,400-degree fireball killed 80,000 and leveled a four-mile-wide circle. The radioactivity spread by the mushroom cloud would claim an estimated 120,000 more lives by 1950.

BERNARD HOFFMAN / LIFE

A Score Is Settled

On the 1,365th day after Pearl Harbor and the 27th after Hiroshima, Japan's leaders ferried across Tokyo Bay to formally surrender on the deck of the USS *Missouri*. The news excited even strangers in Times Square. Yet a lasting peace was no sure thing. America had suffered 300,000 casualties in the Pacific; Japan had lost 4.2 million soldiers and civilians (six percent of its population). But on September 27, Hirohito called on U.S. commander Douglas MacArthur. The emperor, 44, until recently neither seen nor heard by subjects who thought him a god, volunteered to step down. The offer was declined. From this goodwill sprang a benign and mutually beneficial military occupation that would last for seven years.

LEFT: Alfred Eisenstaedt / Life

BELOW: Carl Mydans / Life

STRETCHING TO NEW HEIGHTS

Freed perhaps by the stirring strings that open *Appalachian Spring,* Aaron Copland's 1944 celebration of rural America, Martha Graham, 50, high-kicked loose of the jagged gestures she had championed for two decades. Drawn at 22 to modern dance, Graham's daring choreography and musical tastes prodded her art beyond its classical ballet origins.

JERRY COOKE / LIFE

42 DOWN, 14 TO GO

With this single on June 29, 1941, outfielder Joe DiMaggio, 26, broke George Sisler's modern record of hitting safely in 41 straight games. DiMaggio, known as the Yankee Clipper, would extend the streak to 56 (and lead New York to a World Series title). But Boston's Ted Williams, 23, did even better at the plate, becoming the century's last big leaguer to post a batting average above .400. (He finished the year at .406.)

CORBIS / BETTMANN

SINGER WITH THE SILVER PIPES

Nights were spent at the Paramount in New York City crooning to sold-out crowds of bobby-soxers and days at home in Hoboken, New Jersey, with a pair of Nancys (his first wife, 24, and their firstborn, three). At 26, Frank Sinatra had the world on a string. The singer with the silver pipes and golden phrasing was also a hit in Hollywood. "New York, New York" and "My Way" are two of his many memorable songs.

HERBERT GEHR / LIFE

HIS MAJESTY, THE DUKE

Earlier in 1943, the musicians jamming with Edward Kennedy Ellington, 44, had accompanied him downtown to play at the Carnegie Hall premiere of *Black, Brown and Beige,* his suite to the African-American experience. Nicknamed Duke in high school for his suaveness, Ellington apprenticed at Harlem's Cotton Club before becoming the century's preeminent jazz bandleader and composer.

GJON MILI / LIFE

UNDER WESTERN SKIES

Even as Fermi was experimenting with fission, physicist J. Robert Oppenheimer, 38, and Army general Leslie Groves, who had just finished overseeing construction of the Pentagon, were turning 77 square miles of New Mexico mesa into a top-secret research complex. The army of scientists who came to work at Alamagordo needed almost 26 months to build the first A-bomb. Test date: July 16, 1945.

FRITZ GORO / LIFE

MANHATTAN TRANSFER

Who better in America to test the fission theory than Italian émigré Enrico Fermi, who had just won the 1938 Nobel for physics? He built a reactor beneath the decrepit University of Chicago football stadium (the school had quit the Big Ten). On December 2, 1942, Fermi, 41, and his team achieved a sustained chain reaction. The superbomb was no longer just theory.

NEW YORK HERALD TRIBUNE

Pandora's Box

Though Shakespeare wrote of "atomies," not until the 1930s did anyone suspect that one of nature's tiniest building blocks harbored energy of undreamt scope. War has a way of both hastening and mutating technology; Alfred Nobel cooked up dynamite to help farmers clear tree stumps. The fallout from the only two A-bombs dropped in anger will not dissipate. One casualty: nuclear energy, an industry undone by a string of accidental meltdowns. Another: our psyches. Forget disarmament. We know that those early bombs are puny next to what now fits in a terrorist's valise. But like the genie, knowledge cannot be returned.

WHAT HIS MIND FORESAW

When Albert Einstein, 59, posed here in 1938, scientists in the U.S., England, France and Germany were racing to unlock the secrets of the atom. The next January, a German team came upon a process, fission, that could in theory transform uranium into a superbomb. When Einstein — a Jewish Nobel Laureate who upon Hitler's rise in 1933 had fled to the U.S. — learned of the news, he alerted the White House. In mid-1940, FDR responded by setting up the hush-hush Manhattan Project. Einstein, ironically, was not asked to join. The physicist, whose $E=mc^2$ fundamentally changed the way man understood his universe, was a known pacifist and Zionist, and thus deemed politically unreliable.

ELIOT ELISOFON

ELEMENTARY DEDUCTIONS

For explaining a phenomenon first observed in 1898 — that the metallic element uranium radiates mysterious particles — Marie and Pierre Curie became, in 1903, the first husband-and-wife Nobel Prize winners. The Polish-born Mme. Curie, 36, coined the word *radioactivity*. But handling radioactive samples led to pernicious anemia, from which she died in 1934. By then, a team at Cambridge University in England, led by Ernest Rutherford, had for the first time split an atom (of nitrogen). And later in the 1930s, America's Ernest Lawrence had progressed from a crude 1930 prototype to an advanced model of his cyclotron, a particle accelerator essential to the new science called nuclear physics.

TIME INC.

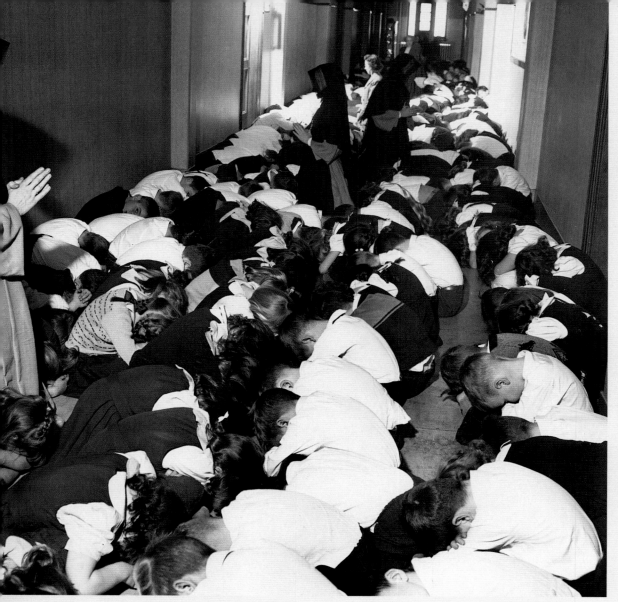

←

IN EVENT OF ATTACK . . .

It was not to pray, but to survive a Red nuclear attack that schoolkids at St. Joan of Arc in Queens huddled in a hall during a civil defense drill in 1951 (two years after the USSR unveiled its first atomic bomb). Also popular: backyard family fallout shelters.

NEW YORK DAILY MIRROR

→

THE CHERNOBYL SYNDROME

Until April 28, 1986, it was a thriller movie plot, not a real concern among nuclear physicists: a runaway reactor that bores straight through the earth to China. Yes, there was that radioactive leak at Three Mile Island, Pennsylvania, but it was minor. Then came the meltdown at Chernobyl, a shoddily built, poorly run Soviet plant in Ukraine. Immediate dead: 31. Long-term dead: 125,000 — and counting.

SHONE / GAMMA LIAISON

7/16/45: TRINITY, NM

A man-made sun usurped the desert dawn — the first A-bomb worked. The test site's name had a biblical ring; yet it was a line from Hinduism's Bhagavad Gita that Robert Oppenheimer recalled: "I am become Death, the destroyer of worlds."

JACK W. AEBY / U.S. ARMY

←

THE DOOMSDAY DEVICES

Replicas of the first two A-bombs sit in a science museum in Los Alamos, New Mexico. Little Boy (far left) was dropped on Hiroshima, Fat Man on Nagasaki four days later, killing 40,000. Why was Germany not also targeted? It had surrendered before the first successful test blast on July 16, 1945.

BEN MARTIN / TIME

BEATRIX POTTER
1866–1943

Love of animals, starting with her own pooch, fills the British writer-illustrator's charming (yet never sentimental) tales. Peter Rabbit debuted in a letter, graced with her own drawings, sent by the 27-year-old Potter to an ailing child. Later would come Squirrel Nutkin, Benjamin Bunny and Jemima Puddle-Duck.

ARCHIVE PHOTOS

LOU GEHRIG
1903–1941

Lured by the New York Yankees from Columbia University, the slugging first baseman (493 career homers) set an endurance mark thought untouchable: 2,130 straight games. It was broken in 1995 (by Cal Ripken Jr.), leaving only a sad medical legacy: Amyotrophic lateral sclerosis, which ended his life, is usually referred to as Lou Gehrig's disease.

AP / WIDE WORLD

F. SCOTT FITZGERALD
1896–1940

Through novels about careless strivers, the Minnesotan earned the social and material success he craved. Fitzgerald and his writer wife, Zelda, were happy to be role models for flapperdom, the time's materialistic, untraditional lifestyle. But his masterpiece, *The Great Gatsby,* foreshadowed the collapse of both the Jazz Age and the couple. She was institutionalized for schizophrenia; he drifted into alcoholism.

TIME INC.

REQUIEM

GEORGE WASHINGTON CARVER
1861–1943

Born a slave in Missouri, he set out at 12 in quest of an education. Two decades later, the agricultural chemist was at Tuskegee Institute, devising new uses for then-unpopular crops like peanuts. By promoting crop diversification — planting a variety of crops on the same land — Carver altered farming worldwide.

SPREADING THE WEALTH

1946 – 1963

To Fulton, Missouri, on March 5, 1946, came President Harry Truman, 62, and former British prime minister Winston Churchill, 72, smoking a cigar. Churchill, the man who willed Britain through the war, had stunningly been voted from office 11 weeks after V-E Day. But he had not lost his grasp of world politics. In a speech that day, Churchill alluded to the policies of the USSR in postwar Europe. He warned, "An iron curtain has descended across the Continent."

GEORGE SKADDING / LIFE

CHANGES

by Patricia and Fredrick McKissack

For those of us who were born during World War II and grew up "colored" in the segregated South during the 1950s, the March on Washington was a defining moment. Although the Supreme Court had ruled in the 1954 landmark case *Brown* v. *Board of Education of Topeka* that segregated schools were unconstitutional, African-American children in 1963 continued to attend predominately segregated schools that were poorly equipped, understaffed and overcrowded. In 1955, Governor George Wallace had stood in the doorway of the University of Alabama to block the passage of a black student, Autherine Lucy, and declared that there would be "segregation today, tomorrow and forever!" Two years later, nine students had to be escorted by federal troops past a yelling mob, surrounding Central High School in Little Rock, Arkansas. And even though the High Court had ruled that segregation on public buses was illegal in 1956 — bringing the Montgomery bus boycott to a successful end — blacks were systematically denied access to higher-paying jobs and decent housing because of discriminatory practices.

Therefore, on August 28, 1963, more than 200,000 people of myriad races, religions and social backgrounds peacefully assembled on the Mall in front of the Lincoln Memorial in the nation's capital to demonstrate that it was time for America to make a change.

Of all the comments made that day, the Reverend Dr. Martin Luther King's "I Have a Dream" speech is the one most remembered. King was a charismatic orator who rallied and unified people under his nonviolent banner and led them in a moral crusade against segregation — though racism and discrimination continue.

The spirit and passion behind the March had been developing since the end of World War II. Returning servicemen were encouraged to attend college, buy houses and take out small business loans with help from the GI Bill passed in 1944. By taking advantage of new opportunities in retail sales, manufacturing and advertising, white veterans built careers that moved them into the swelling ranks of the middle class. By 1950, World War II veterans who had grown up in the Depression had never had it so good — right down to the gray flannel suit, white shirt and dark tie they were *expected* to wear to work.

Except for a few notable exceptions such as Jackie Robinson, the first African-American to sign with a major baseball team, in 1946, and United Nations adviser Dr. Ralph Bunche, winner of the 1950 Nobel Peace Prize, other black professionals were restricted to doing business within their own communities.

Americans felt that the real threat to world peace and security at that time was the uncontrolled spread of communism, led by the Soviet Union and China. Communist North Korea's invasion of South Korea led to military action by the United Nations in 1950. By an executive order issued by President Harry S Truman, black and white American soldiers fought in integrated units for the first time.

Then in 1952, General Dwight D. Eisenhower ran for president, promising to bring the boys home. He won by a landslide and made good his promise. That same year, Malcolm X became actively involved in the Nation of Islam. He became a voice for the poor, black urban masses who, unlike many Southern blacks, could vote but felt they had no reason to vote.

Meanwhile, the Cold War between the Soviet Union and the United States made the world an unstable place, especially when both superpowers were armed with nuclear weapons. Communism and the threat of mass destruction were so frightening that it drove some people to extremes.

Senator Joseph McCarthy made an erroneous claim that the government had been infiltrated by

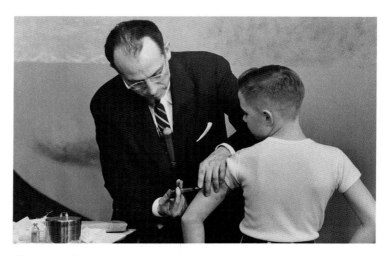

END OF A SCOURGE

In April 1955, Dr. Jonas Salk, 40, of Pittsburgh injected a schoolboy with his newly approved vaccine against the highly contagious disease polio. It was the culmination of eight years of research and field trials (first human guinea pig: himself). Salk's dead-virus vaccine, as well as Alfred Sabin's more effective live-virus version, approved in 1960, virtually wiped out the childhood scourge.

ALBERT FENN / LIFE

hundreds of spies. Investigations led to people being convicted by rumor and hearsay. Although the Senate voted 67–22 to condemn McCarthy's actions, it did very little to help those whose reputations had been ruined.

By the middle of the decade, the nation had experienced a lot of changes. The booming postwar economy had soared to record highs, as had the birthrate. So many children were born between 1946 and 1960 that they were called the "baby boomers." Their parents had married young and would most likely stay together. Their mothers didn't work, and those who did earned half the wages men did, very often for doing the same job.

Children were being born healthier and stronger, and they stayed well because of advancements in pediatric care. A new polio vaccine developed by Dr. Jonas Salk helped save millions of lives. This generation of kids was the first to enjoy hearing *The Cat in the Hat* by Dr. Seuss, play with a Hula Hoop, read Charles M. Schulz's *Peanuts* in the daily newspaper, eat a McDonald's hamburger and experience the wonder and surprise of Disneyland. But nothing was more innovative or revolutionary than television.

Instead of listening to the Lone Ranger on radio, kids could see him and also enjoy Howdy Doody in their living rooms. Their older siblings — now called teenagers — rushed home to watch Dick Clark's *American Bandstand* and dance to the latest rock 'n' roll songs by Chuck Berry, Little Richard or Elvis Presley. Two of the most popular shows in early television were *I Love Lucy* and *The Ed Sullivan Show.* Sullivan endeared himself to millions of teenagers who got a chance to see Elvis perform — even though they saw only the top half of him. His hip-swiveling dancing was considered offensive to most adults. In fact, rock 'n' roll was

BIRTH OF THE BIG MAC

Why were the owners of a single San Bernardino, California, drive-in ordering so many milk-shake makers from him? In 1954, Ray Kroc, 52, flew out to learn that the McDonald brothers — Richard, 45, and Maurice, 52 — were franchising their innovative fast-food techniques. An impressed Kroc bought in and later paid the burger kings $2.7 million for all rights.

CORBIS / BETTMANN

called "the devil's music," or another plot of the Communists to destroy American democracy.

Advertising on television was a natural for the automotive industry. To accommodate the increased number of cars on the road, the federal government began building highways in 1957.

By the late 1950s, there was uneasiness among the war babies that were now coming of age. They were not willing to accept the status quo, and their parents wondered why. Was it the music? Was it the fault of Hollywood's image-makers: sexy Marilyn Monroe, glamorous Elizabeth Taylor, handsome Gregory Peck and the defiant James Dean? Or did it have something to do with *Sputnik,* the first space satellite launched by the Soviets in 1957? In reality, American youth were beginning to question the nation's values. They didn't like what they saw. They were rebels waiting for a cause. At that time few people had even heard of Vietnam.

Beginning in 1960, black and white college students united to participate in sit-ins at lunch counters throughout the South in nonviolent protests against the practice of refusing to serve black customers. Although the students remained peaceful, those who opposed them often resorted to violence. As Americans watched their children being beaten and arrested by police officers, they were disturbed and angered. Stirred by the anthem "We Shall Overcome," adults joined the civil rights movement, even if just by sending a check to an organization. Those who were fearful of change tried to stop the protests or, worse, did nothing.

Later, Betty Friedan's book *The Feminine Mystique* caused young women to examine their own lack of equal rights. The feminist movement began on a much quieter note but would escalate in years to come.

Then on November 8, 1960, John F. Kennedy was elected by a very narrow margin against Richard M. Nixon. But the Kennedys represented the shifting mood of the country. They were young, attractive and stylish. They opened up the doors of the White House to all who caught the vision and believed that they could make a difference. Kennedy asked the National Aeronautics and Space Administration (NASA) to put a man on the moon by the end of the decade. And when John Glenn orbited the earth in the Mercury spacecraft in 1962, space travel changed from science fiction to science. Kennedy also inspired America's youth to join the Peace Corps and work to uplift the poor and downtrodden. But the building of the Berlin Wall and the Bay of Pigs debacle of 1961 and the Cuban missile crisis of 1962 were reminders of how close we lived to a nuclear holocaust.

After the March on Washington, people went home feeling empowered and hopeful. But in September four little black girls were killed in a church bombing in Birmingham, Alabama. While the nation was still recovering from this senseless act of violence, President John F. Kennedy was assassinated in Dallas, Texas, on November 22, 1963. Jack Ruby shot down the suspected assassin, Lee Harvey Oswald, in front of live television cameras. And the nation mourned along with Mrs. Kennedy and her small children their, and our, great loss.

Mercifully the year ended. The highs and lows of 1963 had changed all of us who lived through it. We had remained hopeful in spite of our fears and frustrations. But we'd also learned another important truth — something that our parents had tried to shield us from. Now we knew that not all stories would have a happy ending.

PUTTING OUT THE FIRE OF PROTEST

Some Deep South cities used police clubs, others tear gas. In 1963, Birmingham, Alabama, turned fire hoses on civil rights protesters. The violence displayed by the police against the peaceful protesters backfired. Not only did it fail to stop the protesters, the shocking display helped earn sympathy and support for the growing civil rights movement.

CHARLES MOORE / BLACK STAR

Patricia and Fredrick McKissack are the authors of many books for children, including two Coretta Scott King Award–winning titles, Christmas in the Big House, Christmas in the Quarters *and* A Long Hard Journey, *which also won a Jane Addams Children's Book Award. Ms. McKissack's* The Dark-Thirty: Southern Tales of the Supernatural *won both a Coretta Scott King Award and a Newbery Honor, and her* Mirandy and Brother Wind *was a Caldecott Honor book.*

CRIMES AND PUNISHMENTS

The Allies put 24 Nazis and 28 Japanese leaders (including Hideki Tojo, center) on trial. Beyond reach were Hitler, dead by his own hand, and Italy's Mussolini, shot sneaking back to Milan, where his corpse was hung in public; Japanese emperor Hirohito escaped judgment by using his supreme majesty to ensure a peaceful U.S. occupation of his nation. At Nuremberg, Germany, a number of Nazi leaders were sentenced to death by hanging or life imprisonment. At Tokyo, Prime Minister Tojo, 64 — who the previous September had shot himself in the chest but survived — was hanged in 1948.

CARL MYDANS / LIFE

A YOUNG DIARIST-TO-BE

A slim volume that appeared in Dutch bookstores in 1947 was written by the girl who is second from left in this snapshot taken 10 years before. But in 1942, she and her family, which was Jewish, had to hide in Nazi-occupied Amsterdam. They were betrayed in 1944; she died, at 15, in Bergen-Belsen, a Nazi concentration camp. The slim volume was Anne Frank's heartbreaking diary of those two years in hiding. (Three of her playmates shown here survived the Holocaust.)

ILSE LEDERMAN

OPERATION RESCUE

Flying over a part of Berlin still in ruins in 1948, a USAF C-54 plane arrived full of cargo. In June, the USSR had cut all land and river links to the city, which lay 110 miles inside East Germany. Berlin had been excepted from the four occupation zones created in the wake of World War II because it was the capital of Germany. In 1948, the USSR decided that all of Berlin should be under its control. Western powers disagreed. To supply 2.5 million Berliners with life's necessities, America and Britain began an airlift that averaged 625 flights daily for 318 days.

CHARLES F. JACOBS / BLACK STAR

MARSHALL'S PLAN

As a five-star general, he helped plot the Allied victory. In 1947, as Secretary of State, George C. Marshall, 67, toured Europe, then proposed a reconstruction plan that could run $20 billion over four years. Congress didn't blink and said yes.

THOMAS D. MCAVOY / LIFE

CALL HIM SKY KING

That sharp clap of a sonic boom over California on October 14, 1947, came from this jet piloted by this cockpit stud, Chuck Yeager, 24. The plane (named for his wife) was the first craft to fly faster than the speed of sound under its own power. Some had feared the X-1 might disintegrate. When it passed 700 mph and didn't, gone was the barrier to the jet age in military and commercial flight.

CORBIS / BETTMANN-UPI

→

ONE IS A LONELY NUMBER

Jackie Robinson (here, stealing home in 1948) was the object of much attention — and name-calling. The UCLA graduate had been chosen by general manager Branch Rickey of the Brooklyn Dodgers to break the national pastime's color barrier. Pro football had already accepted black fullback Marion Motley of the Cleveland Browns, and the baseball sage knew that a number of Negro League players, among them, Robinson, could help his team. Rickey couldn't have been more right. Robinson's 1947 debut with the Dodgers helped win them the National League pennant, and Robinson won Rookie of the Year. By 1953, six of the 16 big league teams were suiting up blacks. Last to integrate: the Boston Red Sox, who called up Pumpsie Green in 1959.

HY PESKIN / LIFE

THE TOP OF HER GAME

At 18, Billie Jean Moffit (later Billie Jean King) already held a major title (doubles at Wimbledon). She went on to collect 10 Wimbledon and U.S. Open singles crowns. She became the first woman athlete to earn $100,000 in a year (1971), proving to girls that sweat could be beautiful.

BRIAN SEED / SPORTS ILLUSTRATED

←

VOYAGE OF THE DAMNED

The postwar destination of many vessels packed with displaced Jews (like the ragtag *Szold,* here), was Palestine — biblical Israel. All were turned away by the British, overseers of the territory since 1922. The cruel 1947 rejection of the ship *Exodus,* recounted in a book and a film, turned international public opinion against London. On May 14, 1948, the modern state of Israel was founded as a homeland for world Jewry.

DAVID DOUGLAS DUNCAN

A PASSAGE FROM INDIA

By ending its 89-year colonial rule of India in 1947, Britain washed its hands of the violent, age-old rivalry between Hindus and Muslims. Partitioning off the new state of Pakistan for minority Muslims set off more violence. Most prominent of the million-plus victims: Mohandas Gandhi, assassinated in 1948 by a fellow Hindu for his pacifist, nonpartisan views.

MARGARET BOURKE-WHITE / LIFE

TWO-PIECE BOMBSHELL

Itsy-bitsy teeny-weeny, the Louis Réard creation wasn't. Still, a stunned Paris fashion press was quick to dub it "bikini," after the island in the Pacific where the U.S. tested nukes. Starchy French resorts insisted on one-piece suits. Along the Riviera, they complied by removing the tops.

NINA LEEN / LIFE

WELCOME TO THE BURBS

The new instant community outside Los Angeles (below) was one of a rash put up by developers in the immediate postwar years. In Long Island's Levittown, two bedrooms and a slice of lawn could be had for $6,990. Growing up in such tract houses would not affect speech patterns until, like, wow, the 1980s?

LOOMIS DEAN / LIFE

CRY, THE BELOVED COUNTRY

Historically, South Africa's 11 million nonwhites shared few of the rights enjoyed by the nation's 2.5 million whites. In 1948, after parliament was won by ultrasegregationists, they had even fewer. The harsh new law of the land, called apartheid, regulated every facet of nonwhite life, from public facilities (here, an oceanside bench in Durban) to marriage (not with a white).

N. R. FARBMAN / LIFE

New Land War in Asia

The refugees streaming into Yongdungpo, near Seoul, in 1951 revealed the war destroying their country. Korea had been freed from a long Japanese occupation in 1945 — only to be split at the 38th parallel in 1948. The North (capital: P'yŏngyang) fell under Soviet rule, while the South (capital: Seoul) became a republic. On June 25, 1950, the North mounted a massive invasion. Two weeks later, the U.N.'s first multinational police force — at that time, 18,000 troops provided by the U.S. — began landing at Pusan. Douglas MacArthur, 70, was recalled to duty to head the force, which won back lost territory and drove into the North. But in November, Communist China entered the fray; soon, U.S. troops were retreating south down the mountainous peninsula. Combat seesawed into 1951, with American air power partially checked by the new Soviet MiG-15 fighter jet. In April, when MacArthur vowed to cross the Yalu River to fight Chinese troops in China, Truman fired him. Truce talks, begun in late 1951, were finally concluded in mid-1953. Four million lives were claimed in the three-year undeclared war — 54,000 of them American. At century's end, there was still no peace.

Carl Mydans / Life

Everybody Loves Lucy

In 1948, 99.9 percent of American households were without television. Shows starring Milton Berle and Ed Sullivan quickly helped change this. In 1951, to coax Lucille Ball to TV, CBS met two demands. Real-life hubby Desi Arnaz, Cuban accent and all, would be in the sitcom (with Vivian Vance, left, and William Frawley, far right). And though most other network shows originated live from New York, Ball, 40, would stay in L.A. and do her shows on film. This meant *I Love Lucy*'s slapstick comedy could be sharpened by editing — and its episodes could be rerun for all time.

CBS Photo Archive

→

Long Lives the Queen

She was ten years old when Edward VII gave up the throne and the scepter shifted to her father. At 25, she became Queen of Great Britain and Northern Ireland. Elizabeth II's Coronation Day wave in 1953 was mirrored by her children, Charles, four, and Anne, two. (Andrew would be born in 1960, and Edward in 1964.) In 1996, her reign surpassed Elizabeth I's to become the fifth longest in British history.

Frank Scherschel / Life

Semi-Fast Food

When U.S. stores began to stock a new frozen-food product in 1954, television had penetrated into 26 million households, up from 172,000 in 1948. TV dinners took only 25 minutes to cook and tasted like it.

Courtesy of Swanson Dinners

A BLOODY REGIME ENDS

On Joseph Stalin's 29-year watch, purges and planned famines killed more Soviets than did World War II. So no one was too sad in March 1953 as Kremlin officials bore away the 73-year-old dictator's body. After five years of savage infighting among his successors, one leader emerged: earthy Ukrainian Nikita Khrushchev, 64.

LIFE

SPY TRIAL OF THE CENTURY

In 1950, eight Americans were charged with passing Manhattan Project secrets to Moscow. Three pleaded guilty and were put in jail with the three who were convicted by juries. Remaining were New Yorkers Julius Rosenberg, an electrical engineer, and his homemaker wife, Ethel. Both were acknowledged leftists. Though many at the time thought the government's case left room for reasonable doubt, they alone were condemned to die. The sentences led to a flood of calls for leniency, but the Rosenbergs were executed on June 19, 1953; she was 37, he was 35.

AP

IT'S IN OUR GENES

American biophysicist James Watson, 25 (left), looked on at a May 1953 session during which he and English colleague Francis Crick, 36, explained what they had built. It was a model of deoxyribonucleic acid, the molecule carrying the genetic code that enables cells to replicate. The structure of DNA, they had determined, was a double helix, or spiral. Their find would ripple through worlds as diverse as medicine, agriculture and criminology.

BARRINGTON BROWN / PHOTO RESEARCHERS

ON TOP OF THE WORLD

The air was much thinner where they had recently been: atop Mount Everest's 29,028-foot summit. On May 29, 1953, Edmund Hillary, 33 (left), of New Zealand and Tenzing Norgay, 39, a Sherpa of Nepalese descent, became the first to stand on the planet's highest point. They admired the Himalayan view for 20 minutes, then started the long, dangerous trek back down. Today, people are still obsessed with reaching the summit. The lucky ones live to tell about it.

JAMES BURKE / LIFE

WITCHHUNT

Not since its colonial days had the U.S. been so divided by suspicion. The enemy: a disease called communism. The anticapitalist world according to Marx had never been popular in America; in the late Teens, the rise of Bolshevism set off a Red scare. Postwar, as an Iron Curtain sliced across Europe, the stakes seemed even higher. In 1947, the House of Representatives redefined un-American behavior and found Hollywood full of it. Next, the one-two punch of the Rosenbergs and Korea. If Stalin could steal our atomic secrets, and Beijing and P'yŏngyang our young men's lives, what was left to safeguard but our hearts and minds?

SUFFER THE CHILDREN

It was not the classroom her parents wanted for Linda Brown, 10 (wearing scarf). But a school 17 blocks nearer their Topeka, Kansas, home was whites only. The Browns sued the school board in 1952. On May 17, 1954, the nine white justices of the U.S. Supreme Court ruled that in "public education, the doctrine of separate but equal has no place." The decision would affect 11 million white and black students in 17 states.

CARL IWASAKI / LIFE

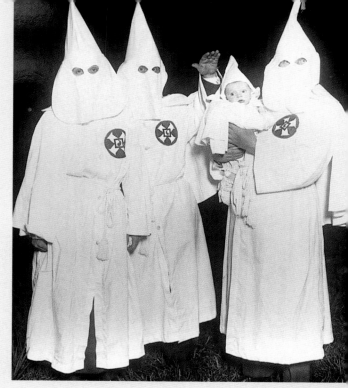

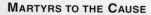

MISSING

THE FBI IS SEEKING INFORMATION CONCERNING THE DISAPPEARANCE
PHILADELPHIA, MISSISSIPPI, OF THESE THREE INDIVIDUALS ON JUNE 21, 1964. EXTENS
NVESTIGATION IS BEING CONDUCTED TO LOCATE GOODMAN, CHANEY, AND SCHWERN
WHO ARE DESCRIBED AS FOLLOWS:

ANDREW GOODMAN	JAMES EARL CHANEY	MICHAEL HENRY SCHWER
White	Negro	White
Male	Male	Male
November 23, 1943	May 30, 1943	November 6, 1939
New York City	Meridian, Mississippi	New York City
20 years	21 years	24 years
5'10"	5'7"	5'9" to 5'10"
150 pounds	135 to 140 pounds	170 to 180 pounds
Dark brown; wavy	Black	Brown
Brown	Brown	Light blue
	Good: none missing	
	1 inch cut scar 2 inches above left ear.	Pock mark center of forehead, slight sca on bridge of nose, appendectomy scar, broken leg scar.

MARTYRS TO THE CAUSE

The three, who were devoting the summer of 1964 to registering rural black Mississippians to vote, were last seen on a dirt road in Neshoba County. They had been stopped for speeding. Six weeks later, their tortured and bullet-riddled corpses were dug up near the town of Philadelphia. Seven locals were convicted, including the chief deputy sheriff of Neshoba County.

CORBIS / BETTMANN-UPI

MARCH ON SELMA

Word obviously had not reached law enforcers in Selma, Alabama, that nine months earlier President Lyndon B. Johnson had signed the Civil Rights Act of 1964. The Act outlawed racial discrimination in many arenas, including banning discriminatory voter registration practices. The Alabama cops soon busted blacks trying to sign up to vote. Those arrests sparked several mass marches. (After one, the KKK shot dead civil rights worker Viola Liuzzo, 38.) That summer, Congress passed the Voting Rights Act of 1965, which reinforced the 1964 act, among other things.

FRANK DANDRIDGE / LIFE

Vigilante Justice

The first Ku Klux Klan was disrobed during the 1870s for its extreme violence. In 1915, William Simmons of Georgia ordered fresh sheets; by the 1920s, the white supremacists totaled four million, mostly in the rural South and Midwest. Also on the rise: lynchings of blacks. The KKK faded during World War II — but would resume night rides in the 1950s as the civil rights movement gained strength.

CORBIS / BETTMANN

Move? Not This Time

She paid the bus fare, so despite local law (blacks to the back of the bus), seamstress Rosa Parks, then 42, decided not to give up her seat to a white man. When she was hauled into court four days later, on December 5, 1955, blacks in Montgomery, Alabama, stopped taking the buses. The boycott, led by the Reverend Martin Luther King Jr., 26, lasted for 381 days, until the Supreme Court struck down the law.

PAUL SCHUTZER / LIFE

They Had a Dream

The first ship bearing Africans to America most likely docked at Jamestown, Virginia, in 1619. From the start, slavery divided the country's whites, who eventually settled their differences in battle. The Civil War freed the nation's blacks. But left intact were the legacies of slavery, the cruelest of which was the perception that skin color mattered. Epic legislation, earned with tears, sweat and blood, has spelled out basic civil rights but not put an end to racism. Which is ironic. If the geneticists have it right, everyone living in the United States is an African-American, descended — like the rest of humanity — from the people who inhabited sub-Saharan Africa 400,000 years ago.

Turning Neither Cheek

W. E. B. Du Bois's 1903 book, *The Souls of Black Folk,* rejected the tolerance of racism favored by Booker T. Washington. In 1910, at 42, the sociologist (Harvard's first black Ph.D.) co-founded the NAACP (National Association for the Advancement of Colored People). Du Bois grew impatient with the movement's slow progress and, late in life, renounced his U.S. citizenship. He died in Ghana one year before the Civil Rights Act of 1964.

CULVER PICTURES

BEAUTIFUL DREAMER

On August 28, 1963, before some 250,000 fellow citizens thronging the Mall in Washington, D.C., and uncounted millions watching on live TV, Martin Luther King Jr., 34, related his vision for a more equitable America. King had flaws. (The FBI gathered personal dirt in an effort to shut him up.) But his strengths — passion, soaring language — pushed the civil rights movement over the top.

FRANCIS MILLER / LIFE

A U.S. BENCHMARK

On October 2, 1967, with a hand from wife Cecilia, Thurgood Marshall, 59, prepared to be sworn in as the Supreme Court's 96th — and first black — justice. His legal views were no mystery to Lyndon Johnson, who named him, nor to the Senate, which confirmed him (by 69–11). Just 14 years earlier, Marshall had stood before the Court to argue the landmark *Brown* v. *Board of Education*.

AP / WIDE WORLD

TIME TO SMELL THE ROSES

Colin Powell, first black to head the Joint Chiefs of Staff (the nation's highest military post), had overseen Operation Desert Storm in the Persian Gulf in 1991. Here, in 1993, with wife Alma he gave the last salute of a 35-year career. When he grew up in New York during World War II, the Army was still segregated. His time to serve was Vietnam (10.5 percent of U.S. troops were black). Courted by the Republicans to run against Bill Clinton in 1996, he declined.

FAMILIAR YET SO NEW

The New York art world was in love with abstract expressionism when Jasper Johns (seated) hit town. In 1954, Johns, 24 (an admirer of Dadaist Marcel Duchamp), began to make deadpan paintings of common icons: the Stars and Stripes, targets, even numbers. A smash 1958 gallery show helped pave the road to Pop Art. In 1999, a Johns fetched $7.1 million at auction.

PETER STACKPOLE / LIFE

A RACE AGAINST TIME

Even Roger Bannister, a medical student as well as a premier British miler, wondered if the human body was built to run a mile in less than four minutes. But on May 6, 1954, the future neurologist, 25, became the first, breaking the tape in 3:59.4.

OXFORD DAILY MAIL

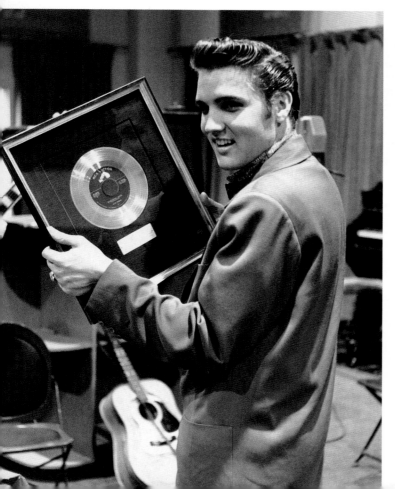

← →

ROLL OVER, BEETHOVEN

The backbeat-driven sound sure riled the geezers, but there was more to it than that. Rock 'n' roll was here to stay. Back in 1947, Les Paul had taken a perfectly good guitar and stuck a cord in it. R&B had been introduced into white mainstream culture. But not until a movie director showcased a failed two-year-old single did rock really start becoming popular. The movie: 1955's *Blackboard Jungle,* about juvenile delinquents. The song: "(We're Gonna) Rock Around the Clock" by Bill Haley and His Comets. The next year, Elvis Aron Presley, 21, of Tupelo, Mississippi (left), went gold with "Heartbreak Hotel." The talented, hip-swinging singer redefined the role of superstar. In 1957, when Dick Clark (right), then 28, launched *American Bandstand* on national TV, not all chart toppers were rock. Soon they were. Clark continued on in an industry that would refuse to age.

LEFT: DON CRAVENS / LIFE

RIGHT: PAUL SCHUTZER / LIFE

A Hit and a Miss

Buoyed by demand for its two-seat Thunderbird (above), unveiled in 1955, Ford went public. Gulp. In 1957, another rollout, developed at a cost of $250 million, caught no one's fancy. Only 110,000 Edsels had been sold when the company pulled the plug on the model.

AUTOMOBILE QUARTERLY

To Catch a Prince

She went to the Riviera to film Hitchcock's *To Catch a Thief* — and caught a prince. In April 1956, Oscar winner Grace Kelly, 26, was wed to Rainier III, 32, ruler of Monaco, a 370-acre principality pirated from France by his Grimaldi forebears in 1297. She instantly brought class to a haven for gamblers and tax cheats once described as "a sunny place for shady people."

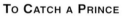
THOMAS D. McAVOY / LIFE

May I Be Your Friend?

With unrealistic body proportions, pals like Ken and Midge, and one billion pairs of shoes and counting, Barbie Millicent Roberts made her debut in time for Christmas, 1959. Girlhood, and family budgets, has never been the same.

AP / WIDE WORLD

COURTING GREATNESS

Surely, growing up in Harlem, Althea Gibson never expected to be celebrated with a ticker tape parade downtown. But in 1957, at 29, she had just become the first black to win a major singles tennis title, Wimbledon. (Nine weeks later, Gibson added the U.S. Nationals, now the Open, crown.) By the time the pro tour took root in the late 1960s, alas, her game was past its prime.

CORBIS / BETTMANN-UPI

BEFORE THE FALL

She went from nude calendars to Hollywood "B" icon: the breathless, brainless blonde whom gentlemen preferred. Marilyn Monroe sought more. In choicer roles, as in 1959's *Some Like It Hot,* she proved herself one funny lady. Personal happiness was harder. After marriages to, among others, Joe DiMaggio and playwright Arthur Miller (above), she entered hapless affairs with, among others, U.S. President John F. Kennedy, before OD'ing on drugs in 1962, at age 36.

PAUL SCHUTZER / LIFE

145

JUST ONE WORD: PLASTICS

The Hula Hoop–challenged were in the minority in 1958; 25 million were sold, at $1.98 each, before the fad wound down. The previous year, the same company, Wham-O, had introduced another polystyrene novelty that would have more hang time: the Pluto Platter (soon renamed Frisbee).

ARTHUR SHAY / LIFE

SUDDEN DEATH, NEW LIFE

It may not have been the greatest pro football game ever, but Colts vs. Giants on December 28, 1958, was the most important. The NFL championship riveted TV fans through four quarters — plus 8:15 of the first overtime in league history (final: Baltimore 23, New York 17). Madison Avenue decided the sport was hot; CBS locked in a long-term contract; and in 1960, ABC helped fund a rival league, the AFL.

HY PESKIN / SPORTS ILLUSTRATED

ENCORE, MON GENERAL?

A chaotic France in 1958 reached back into history for help. Heeding the call: 6'4" Charles de Gaulle. In World War II he led the Free French movement from exile. A string of weak governments since then had let slip France's colonial empire. (Vietnam bid adieu in 1954, North Africa was now in open revolt.) To restoré calm, De Gaulle, 67, demanded extraordinary powers. He was granted them.

CORBIS / BETTMANN-UPI

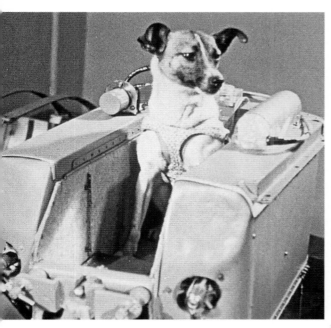

CANINE ASTRONAUT

On October 4, 1957, the USSR launched into orbit *Sputnik I,* the first man-made satellite. The second, set for November 3, carried a passenger: a *laika* (not its name, but rather the Russian word for various husky breeds). The 13-pound dog survived its ride into space aboard *Sputnik II;* the trip, alas, was one-way.

SOVFOTO

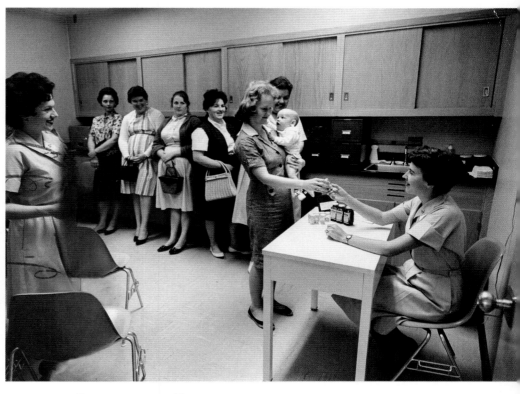

PRESENTING THE PILL

Women of childbearing age lined up at a public clinic in Charlotte, North Carolina, for the first birth-control pill to win Food and Drug Administration approval (in 1960). Enovid 10, a mix of the hormones progesterone and mestranol, was developed by endocrinologist Gregory Pincus and tested by gynecologist John Rock.

JIM MAHAN / LIFE

A Vote for Independence

Almost four years after France called on Charles de Gaulle to solve its Algerian crisis, the North African colony was still a battle zone. Refusing to let go was a coalition of longtime colonizers and right-wingers in France itself. De Gaulle finally set a pullback for mid-1962. Some 1.4 million Europeans fled Algeria while the Muslim majority voted to ratify the nation's independence.

DALMAS-SIPA PRESS

Castro in Control

The man being cheered in Cienfuegos, Cuba, on January 8, 1958, was *muy importante:* At 31, lawyer turned rebel Fidel Castro had won control of his Caribbean nation after a three-year guerrilla war to oust Mafia-corrupted dictator Fulgencio Batista. Castro said he was an anti-imperialist, not a Communist. Who knew?

GREY VILLET / LIFE

BRICK BY BRICK

In August 1961, GIs and East German troops confronted each other across the crude wall being built by the Communists to bisect Berlin. Reason: Too many East Germans were fleeing to the West via the Allied-run sector of this partitioned city. The Wall was an instant Iron Curtain icon; in 1963, it played a key role in John le Carré's breakthrough thriller, *The Spy Who Came In from the Cold.* The wall was torn down in 1989.

PAUL SCHUTZER / LIFE

COME ON, BABY . . .

That was no typical rock crowd packing a Hollywood club in 1961, but fans of America's hottest singer, Ernest Evans, a.k.a. Chubby Checker, 20 (showing a fan how to do the new fad, the Twist). An easy step for the Hula Hoop generation, it set off an intense, but brief, spate of weird dances, such as the Bristol Stomp, the Loco-Motion and the Freddie.

RALPH CRANE / LIFE

Space Pioneer

The first human in space: Soviet cosmonaut Yuri Gagarin, 27 (left center), two days after his April 12, 1961, mission. He was on the podium by invitation of the proud man to his left, Soviet premier Nikita Khrushchev. Gagarin's craft, *Vostok I,* hit 17,400 mph on the 89-minute flight. That May 5, astronaut Alan Shepard Jr., 37, became the first American in space. He rode *Freedom 7* to an altitude of 115 miles but did not orbit the planet, as had Gagarin. Although the U.S. was playing catch-up, President John F. Kennedy, known as JFK, boldly vowed to put an American on the moon by the end of the decade.

JAMES WHITMORE / LIFE

But the Model Was Cheap

Cézanne painted a wine bottle, and no one blinked. Yet people howled at the canvases of Andy Warhol (painted in 1963, when the Pittsburgh native was 35). That many of his works seemed straight out of a supermarket flyer was precisely the point; if nothing else, Pop Art was fueled by artistic irony.

THE ANDY WARHOL FOUNDATION / ART RESOURCE

DESTINATION: CUBA. COURSE: COLLISION

At their first summit, in 1961 in Vienna, Khrushchev judged John F. Kennedy (inset) to be weak. The next summer, he began arming new ally Fidel Castro with medium-range ballistic missiles. On October 14, a U.S. spy plane photographed launch sites under construction. On the 22nd, JFK ordered an air and sea quarantine of Cuba. It took six days of angry negotiations, by way of intermediaries, letters and telexes, before Khrushchev caved and agreed to take back the weapons. (Here, a Soviet freighter carrying home missiles was escorted by a U.S. warship.) Shaken by their close brush with nuclear war, the superpowers, in 1963, installed a hot line between Moscow and Washington.

CARL MYDANS / LIFE

INSET: ARTHUR RICKERBY / LIFE

YOU SAY YOU WANT A REVOLUTION . . .

Band's name? Cute. New drummer? Seems to be working out. Haircuts and stage attire? Need work. Footwear? Puleeeze! The year was 1963, the venue Liverpool's Cavern Club. John Lennon, 22, George Harrison, 20, Paul McCartney, 21, and Ringo Starr, 22, were doing fab in Europe. Most Americans, though, thought a Beatle was a German car — until January 1964, that is, when "I Want to Hold Your Hand" crossed the Pond. The Beatles went on to record more than 30 songs that hit *Billboard*'s top-ten list.

THE LION WEEPS TONIGHT

The old folkies' home beckoned hum-and-strum acts like the Kingston Trio after a 1963 folk concert in Newport, Rhode Island, led by Joan Baez, 22, and Bob Dylan, 22. As if sensing which way the Sixties were blowin', the writer-singers revived the social consciousness of such fabled balladeers as Joe Hill, Woody Guthrie and the Weavers.

WONDERFUL WILT THE STILT

Bevo Francis and Frank Selvy did it against hapless college foes. But no pro scored 100 points in one game until March 2, 1962, when 7'1" Philadelphia Warrior Wilt Chamberlain, 26, eased in points 99 and 100 against the New York Knicks in Hershey, Pennsylvania. Next best NBA single night's work: Wilt with 78 points.

AP / WIDE WORLD

DEATH OF A PRESIDENT

JFK, 46, wanted to mend a few political fences in Dallas before the 1964 election; His wife, Jacqueline Bouvier Kennedy, 34, had joined him despite her distaste for politics. They set off by car for a rally downtown. At high noon, the motorcade passed through Dealey Plaza. From the sixth floor of a warehouse on the square rang three shots. The last bullet shattered the president's head; 30 minutes later, he was pronounced dead. Dallas police soon arrested a warehouse worker. Lee Harvey Oswald, 24, was a troubled ex-Marine marksman who after quitting the corps tried, in vain, to become a Soviet citizen. The day after Oswald's arraignment, he was slain — on live TV — by Jack Ruby, a Dallas strip-joint owner with mob ties. Even as conspiracy theories emerged to explain this stunning series of improbable events, Mrs. Kennedy was back in Washington, burying her husband.

ABOVE: ART RICKERBY / LIFE

RIGHT: BOB JACKSON / DALLAS TIMES HERALD

←

EVA PERÓN
1919–1952

Her acting won no praise, but it led the Buenos Aires native out of poverty and into the plum role of First Lady of Argentina. Evita's generous social programs endeared her to the masses and sealed support for dictator husband Juan. Her own loyalty was boundless. Left too weak from cancer to stand, she was once wired-and-plastered upright. She then camouflaged the brace under her flowing mink coat.

MICHAEL ROUGIER / LIFE

→

FRANK LLOYD WRIGHT
1867–1959

Forging a distinctly American style of architecture was Wright's quest. Here, he is at Taliesin West, his winter home and studio in Arizona. Though an early advocate of mass-produced construction materials, he had a gift for making buildings seem to emerge organically from their sites. A house named Fallingwater in Bear Run, Pennsylvania, included a section extending over a waterfall. He also designed 20 "prairie houses" in the Chicago area. His love of free-flowing interiors is evident in New York City's spiraling Guggenheim Museum.

ALLAN GRANT / LIFE

BILLIE HOLIDAY
1915–1959

The self-taught singer overcame a grim childhood in Baltimore to reign as the supreme jazz vocalist of her era. Lady Day toured with the bands of Count Basie and Artie Shaw and, with saxophonist Lester Young, cut a stack of LPs good enough to stand the test of time. Her own time came too early: She was a casualty of heroin.

GJON MILI / LIFE

→

JIM THORPE
1888–1953

Jim Thorpe's parents were of Sauk and Fox ancestry, and his given name was Wa-tho-huck, meaning "Bright Path." A football All-American at Carlisle Indian Industrial School in Pennsylvania, he also won the pentathlon and decathlon at the 1912 Stockholm Games — only to forfeit the medals after it was learned he had played semipro baseball. Those golds were restored to Thorpe's family in 1984. In 1950, nearly 400 sportswriters voted Thorpe the greatest all-around athlete of the first half of the 20th Century.

CULVER PICTURES

ROBERT FROST
1874–1963

Rejected by U.S. publishers, the poet went to London, where, with the help of Ezra Pound, his first book of poetry was released in 1913. By the time he came home, his verses on rural New England had won him fans on both sides of the ocean. Despite his celebration of the farming life, it really wasn't for him: Frost milked his cows at night so he could snooze in the morning.

HOWARD SOCHUREK / LIFE

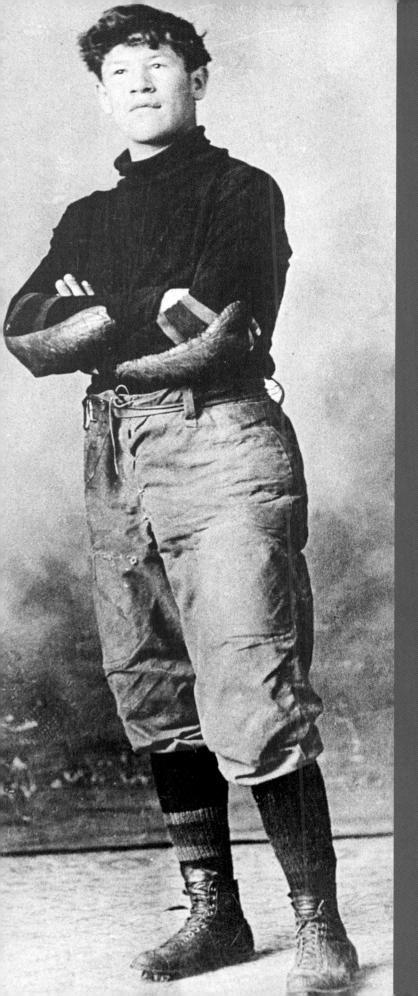

REQUIEM

JAMES DEAN
1931–1955

In life a star, in death he inspired a cult to rival Hollywood's first heartthrob, Rudolph Valentino. The Indiana native began acting in his teens. The brooding explosiveness he projected in live TV dramas and on Broadway led him west to make *East of Eden* and *Rebel Without a Cause*. Dean died in character: He totaled his Porsche before the release of his third and final movie, *Giant.*

1964–1975

After President Nixon ordered GIs into neutral Cambodia, even normally tranquil campuses like Kent State reacted. On May 4, 1970, Ohio National Guardsmen fired tear gas at protesting students, then bullets. The exchange wounded 11 and killed four.

KENT STATE UNIVERSITY ARCHIVES

YEARS OF TURBULENCE

by Jerry Spinelli

How do you sum up a time in which a film about nuclear annihilation *(Dr. Strangelove)* and a TV series called *Happy Days* were equally popular? A time that mixed race riots and *Sesame Street,* death by assassination and go-go dancers?

The diversity of the times was a reflection of its turbulence. Tectonic shifts in society's strata sent quakes of change to the surface. For the first time ever, the United States lost a war. Gas prices soared past a dollar per gallon. Boys and men let their hair grow long. People called streakers dashed naked before vast audiences. Hostesses spiked brownies with psychedelic drugs. A woman (Billie Jean King) beat a man (Bobby Riggs) in tennis on national TV. A black man (Henry Aaron) surpassed Babe Ruth in career home runs. A president (Richard Nixon) resigned. Clothing for men and women merged into something called unisex. But there was still a status quo. There was something for everyone. And something for everyone to be against. There was a lot of protesting. Protestable causes ranged from civil rights to the length of people's hair. A popular form of protest was the so-called be-in. To have a be-in, you gathered a group of like-minded

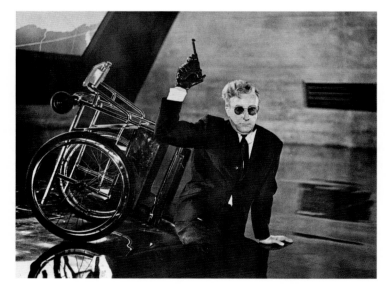

ACHTUNG! WAR IS FUNNY!

Peter Sellers's Dr. Strangelove, title character of the 1964 Stanley Kubrick Cold War satire, is a German now advising the Pentagon ("He's *our* Nazi!"). This lampoon of the nuclear arms race is not subtle; other characters are named Merkin Muffley (also played by Sellers), Buck Turgidson, Bat Guano. But it did uncork a considerable supply of precious bodily fluids — tears of laughter.

ARCHIVE PHOTOS

folks and just sat yourself down someplace that would draw attention to your protest, and maybe get yourself tossed in jail for a few hours as well.

Even war, the ultimate protest, came in an assortment of styles. There was the war in Vietnam, the Cold War and, on the home front, the war for civil rights.

Packed now into a wall memorial in Washington, D.C., the Vietnam War at the time left few in this country untouched. Maybe you joined the Army to go over and fight. Maybe you sweated out the draft call numbers. Maybe you protested because you believed your country had no business meddling in Asian affairs. Maybe you wrote essays in class. Maybe you grieved over someone who came home from the war in a casket.

On May 4, 1970, National Guard troops opened fire on antiwar demonstrators on the campus of Kent State University. Four students were killed. Across the land, 75 colleges called off the rest of the school year. Young people talked of moving to Canada or Sweden. Some did.

In the battle for racial equality, uniforms were issued at birth: your black or white skin. *White* was as white as always, but the word *black* acquired

BRING HOME THE TROOPS!

Not only the usual better-Red-than-dead coalitions opposed U.S. action in Vietnam; these San Franciscans stopped downtown traffic in April 1967. By then, 440,000 Americans were in "Big Muddy," a slang term for Vietnam.

RALPH CRANE / LIFE

new meaning. It replaced the words *Negro* and *colored* as identifiers for African-Americans, who furthermore declared that "black is beautiful."

Not all white-skinned Americans agreed, and since they pretty much ran the country, blacks continued to have limited access to housing, jobs, education, even the voting booth. And so there were riots in city streets, answered by police dogs and water hoses. And peaceful marches, answered by more police dogs and water hoses. And murder in Mississippi. And Malcolm X and Martin Luther King Jr. And assassins' bullets for each of them.

The two wars — domestic and foreign — came together in the flashing fists and mouth of a boxer from Louisville named Cassius Marcellus Clay. In 1964, Cassius Clay won the heavyweight title from Sonny Liston and proclaimed himself "the Greatest!" Most white Americans dismissed his claim as empty boasting. In that year, the worst horrors and bloodshed of the war abroad and racial strife at home were ahead of us. Outside of the ring Clay committed two primary acts of separation and identity: he changed his religion to the Nation of Islam and his name to Muhammad Ali, and he refused

SAIGON FALLS

By April 29, 1975, the U.S. was evacuating its nationals (and a few foreign friendlies) one by one out of Vietnam. The next day, Saigon, scene of this airlift, fell to the Communists, who renamed it Ho Chi Minh City.

HUBERT VAN ES / CORBIS / BETTMANN-UPI

induction into the U.S. Army. The former endeared him to many black Americans, and the latter made him a hero among protesters against the war in Vietnam. By 1975, the foreign war was over, the riots (at least) were over and when Muhammad Ali said he was "the Greatest!" few of any color disagreed.

Then there was the Cold War. America vs. USSR. The Cold War operated on the fascinating notion that there is no surviving a nuclear war, so it's best not to start one in the first place. This was to be accomplished by both sides stacking such great piles of bombs that attack by either side would be mutually suicidal. The result was full employment for the arms makers and nervous tics for the rest of us. The absurdity of the Cold War was captured in the 1964 film satire *Dr. Strangelove,*

or How I Learned to Stop Worrying and Love the Bomb.

While we looked to the sky in fear of nuclear missiles from Moscow, we also looked up in wonder at the achievements of our people in space. Undoubtedly, the popular climax occurred on July 20, 1969, when American astronaut Neil Armstrong became the first person to set foot on the moon.

As astronauts walked routinely on the moon, earthbound shoppers walked the corridors of huge indoor downtowns called malls. We railed at the soaring price of gasoline. We watched TV shows such as *All in the Family* and *The Brady Bunch* and *Laugh-In* and *Star Trek* and the massacre of Israeli athletes at the Munich Olympics on TV. At the movies we saw *The Sound of Music* and *2001: A Space Odyssey* and *The Godfather.* Records of the Beatles and Bob Dylan and Jimi Hendrix spun on our hi-fis and stereos. We doted on media stories of Woodstock and Watergate and President Nixon's resignation. *Sesame Street,* ATMs, Earth Week, *Monday Night Football,* Nike shoes, NutraSweet, the National Organization for Women (NOW), microwave ovens, heart transplants, waterbeds, a video game called Pong: All began during these years.

In November 1973, as the Watergate scandal prompted daily headlines, a spacecraft named

Pioneer 10 sailed past Jupiter, snapping pictures and sending them back to earth. Its main mission achieved, *Pioneer 10* flew on past the other planets and out of the solar system. It sails on today and may well sail on forever, carrying to the stars a special emissary from us all: a golden plaque with etched figures of a man and a woman.

Perhaps in their very simplicity, those figures say what is best about us. As in all times, most people from 1964 to 1975 made neither headlines nor history. They merely carried on the business of being human. Let it be noted, then, that midway through this period of years the following was reported in the January 2, 1970, edition of the Phoenixville, Pennsylvania, *Daily Republican:*

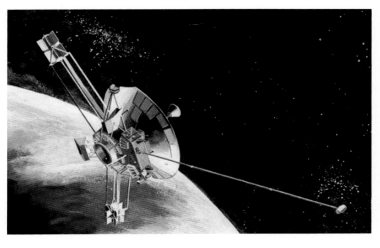

Is Anybody Out There?

On June 13, 1983, 11 years and three months after leaving Earth, the space probe *Pioneer 10* passed Pluto's orbit. A gold-oxidized aluminum plate was attached to the outside of the probe. On the plate were pictures explaining who made the probe (humans) and from what planet it came (Earth). So far, the first man-made object to leave the solar system has not been returned.

NASA/Ames Research Center

Kent State Aftermath

Here lies Jeffrey Miller, one of the four killed when National Guardsmen fired tear gas and bullets at anti–Vietnam War protesters on the usually peaceful campus. The violent deaths shocked the American public. Kneeling next to him is a runaway, later identified as Mary Ann Vecchio, 14. Student strikes and antiwar protests were held on hundreds of college campuses during this time.

John Filo

"The East Vincent Neighbors Club held its annual Christmas covered dish luncheon at the home of Mrs. Walter Scheib, Seven Stars Rd., with 17 members present. After lunch the business meeting was conducted. It was reported that seven fruit baskets were distributed at Thanksgiving to shut-ins in the vicinity."

Jerry Spinelli is the author of the Newbery Medal–winning Maniac Magee, *which also won many other awards. His novel* Wringer *was a Newbery Honor book. Mr. Spinelli's other acclaimed titles include* Space Station Seventh Grade, Who Put That Hair in My Toothbrush?, Jason and Marceline *and* Crash.

He Will Bury Who?

Dust got into Nikita Khrushchev's eye in October 1964. Days later, it was a stick; the Kremlin ousted its premier after six years both turbulent (the Cuban missile crisis) and buffoonish (at a U.N. meeting, he banged on the desk with one of his shoes). Yet Khrushchev, 70, was the first Soviet leader to leave office alive. He and wife Nina finished their days at a country house near Moscow.

Henri Dauman

He Stung Like a Bee

By knocking out Sonny Liston in February 1964, Cassius Clay became, at 22, world heavyweight champ. Soon he embraced the Black Muslim faith and adopted the name Muhammad Ali. But in 1967, upon refusing to be drafted for religious reasons, Ali was stripped of the title. He had to sit out three years. Not until 1974 did he reclaim the crown, by rope-a-doping George Foreman in the "Rumble in the Jungle" in Zaire.

Herb Scharfman / Life

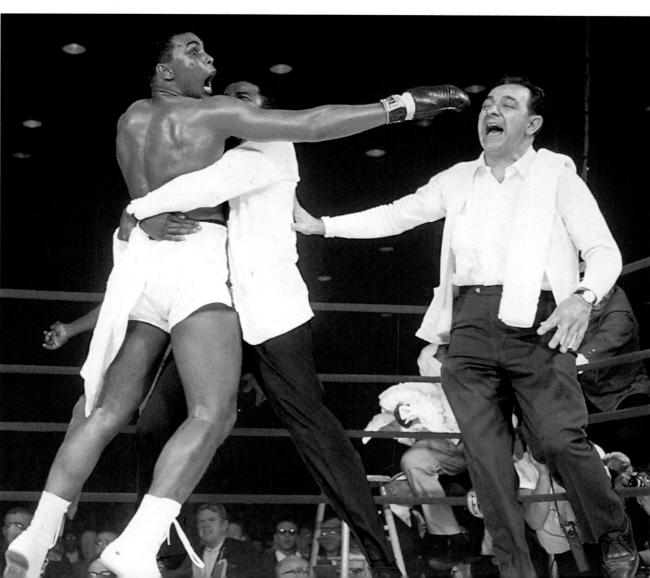

THE STREAM WOULD WIDEN

Captain Vernon Gillespie, on a mission with Vietnamese troops, was, in November 1964, one of 23,000 U.S. advisers training South Vietnam's army. But President Johnson had just won four more years in the White House. He had Congress's O.K. to use "all necessary measures" to contain North Vietnam. By August 1965, there would be 125,000 American troops "in country" — and draft boards would soon be inducting 35,000 men a month.

LARRY BURROWS / LIFE

The Writing on the Wall

In mid-February 1965, he was trying to jump-start his new Organization of Afro-American Unity. Malcolm X, 39 (with wife Betty Shabazz and their daughters), had broken with the Black Muslims over tactics to speed black empowerment. The split proved fatal. At an upcoming rally, three men would shoot him dead.

GREG HARRIS / LIFE

←

Shape of Things To Come

Less than a week after the Voting Rights Act of 1965 became law, a Los Angeleno fell victim to the lawlessness destroying the Watts neighborhood. The poor South-Central neighborhood became a war zone after the August 11 arrest of a black motorist. L.A. riot police couldn't reclaim the streets; 12,500 National Guardsmen needed five days. The toll: 34 dead, 4,000 arrested, damages as high as $200 million.

CO RENTMEESTER

LITTLE (BLOOD-)RED BOOK

To rekindle the spirit that had swept him to power, in 1966 Mao Tse-tung, 72, called for a Cultural Revolution. What he wanted and got was class warfare. His little red book was officially called *Quotations from Chairman Mao* and was meant to inspire. His youthful Red Guards eagerly targeted academics, professionals — and anyone who questioned the absolute wisdom of Mao, the Great Helmsman. Tens of thousands died in the 10-year spasm that cost China its near future.

AP

THE FIRES THIS TIME

Watts was no aberration. Two years later, in 1967, inner cities combusted across America. The worst rioting again sprang from friction between blacks and cops. Detroit police busted an after-hours club; the ensuing week of arson (intentionally burning property) and looting (here, a middle-class black neighborhood) was biracial, but 36 of the 43 dead were black. Newark's police beat a black motorist; the following four days of conflict left 26 dead, 24 of them black. In November, the Census Bureau reported that compared with whites, nonwhites were twice as likely to be unemployed and three times as likely to live in substandard housing.

DECLAUN HAUN / LIFE

FAST WAR, SLOW PEACE

Israel heard the murmurings of war from a coalition of Arab states, so on June 5, 1967, it launched preemptive strikes on Egypt and Syria. Jordan counterattacked. By Day 3, Israel was winning on all fronts (here, Egyptian POWs in the Sinai). On Day 6, the war was over. Israel's reward: the Old City of Jerusalem, site of Judaism's sacred Wailing Wall, won from Jordan. Gravest unintended consequence: From the shattered Arab lands would emerge the militant Palestine Liberation Organization, or PLO.

Denis Cameron

GOOD VIBRATIONS

The AM lyrics in 1967 echoed the tribal desires of young America. Groovin' on a Sunday afternoon. There's a new generation with a new explanation. Come on, baby, light my fire. All you need is love. But the issues of the day would not quit: 128 cities hit by racial rioting, 125,000 antiwar marchers in New York City. This Summer of Love was far from endless.

LYNN PELHAM / LIFE

EASTERN RELIGION IN THE EAST VILLAGE

It was a time for gurus, ashrams and sitars (heard on the Beatles' epic 1967 LP, *Sgt. Pepper's Lonely Hearts Club Band*). But those orange-robed street beggars? Strictly from New York City's East Village, where, at 70, A. C. Bhaktivedanta of Calcutta had begun to chant *hare hare, hare rama,* and so forth. The chant and simple communal Hare Krishna lifestyle were a good trip for many.

VERNON MERRITT / LIFE

Apocalypse 1968

The year began with a reassuring sense of order as coach Vince Lombardi barked the Green Bay Packers to a second Super Bowl title. Nice things did happen (California's Redwood National Park was born). And joyous things (Marvin Gaye's song "I Heard It Through the Grapevine"). And cutting-edge things (the first ATM, in Philadelphia). But mostly, it was bad news on the doorstep. From the growing generation gap there developed a crack that divided along cultural fault lines. The year quickly clenched itself into a fist that never did relax. And the anger still haunts.

Knee Deep in Big Muddy

At year's start, there were 500,000 U.S. combatants in Vietnam. Few expected a 41-city assault by North Vietnamese regulars and Vietcong guerrillas on the lunar new year, called Tet, which occurred on January 30. American casualties ran high at strongholds like Hue. The Tet Offensive achieved little militarily but much politically: It led to enough antiwar opposition to undermine the Johnson presidency. Ordered to step up the peace campaign, GIs commanded by Lieutenant William Calley snapped on March 16 at a hamlet called My Lai. Not until 20 months later was the slaughter of 347 villagers exposed. At Calley's trial, some Americans thought him a hero.

John Olson / Life

Street Justice in Saigon

Day 2 of the Tet Offensive. Suspected Vietcong Bay Lop had already undergone interrogation by South Vietnamese national policemen. One policeman decided to show off the prisoner to the unit's top officer. He was Brigadier General Nguyen Ngoc Loan, 37, whose summary judgment of guilt was captured in a still photograph that revulsed the world. Before his death in 1998, Loan operated a pizza parlor in Dale City, Virginia.

Eddie Adams / AP

RFK (1925–1968)

Robert Francis Kennedy, brother of JFK and former U.S. attorney general, had gone to California to run in the Democratic presidential primary. On June 5, stepping from a victory party in Los Angeles's Ambassador Hotel, the New York senator was struck by three .22 rounds fired point-blank. In 1969, disgruntled Palestinian Sirhan Bishara Sirhan, 25, was convicted of the crime. California abolished the death penalty in 1972; Sirhan's sentence became life imprisonment.

Bill Eppridge / Life

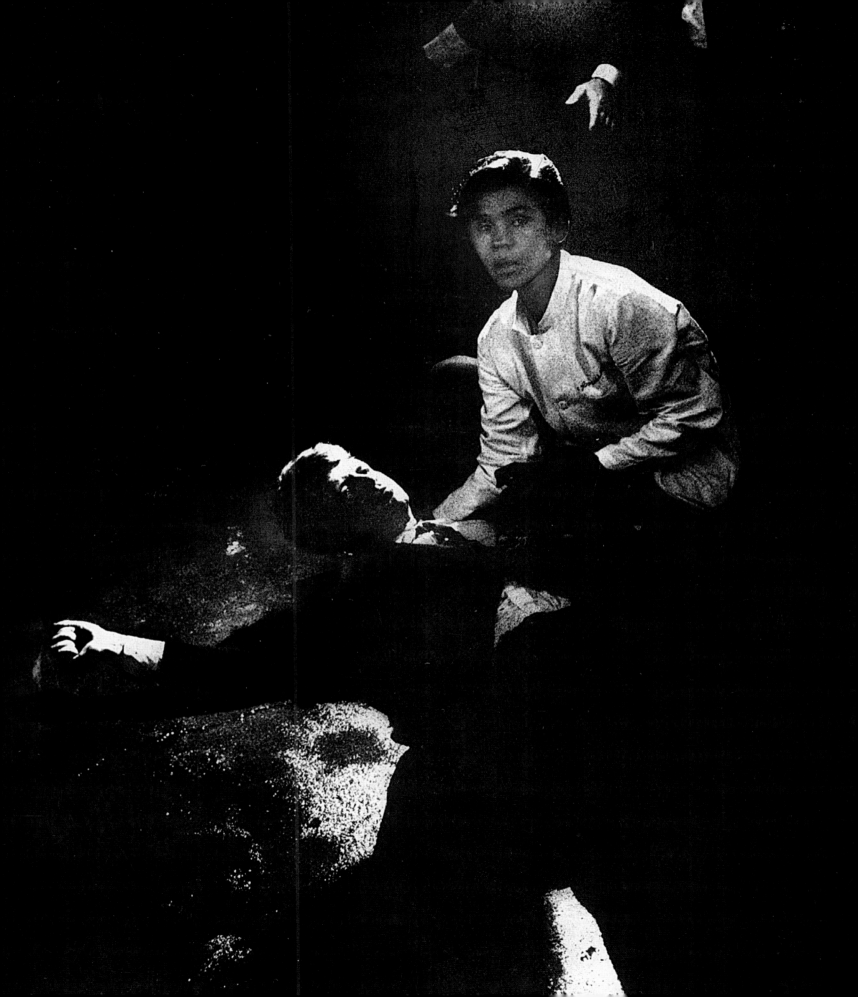

MLK (1929–1968)

Martin Luther King Jr. had gone to Tennessee in support of striking sanitation workers in Memphis. On April 4, stepping from his room at the Lorraine Motel, the civil rights leader was killed by a 30.06 round fired from a nearby boardinghouse. In 1969, escaped con and white supremacist James Earl Ray, 41, was found guilty of the crime; he died in jail in 1998.

JOSEPH LOUW / LIFE

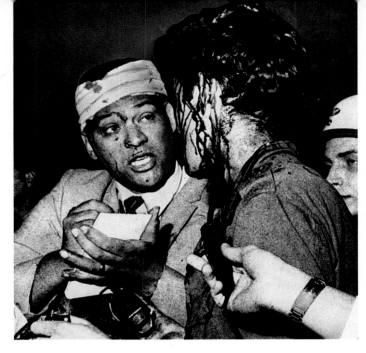

AN UNCONVENTIONAL CONVENTION

John Evans of NBC News ignored his injuries to take notes; the August Democratic National Convention did not lack for stories. Delegates still reeling from President Lyndon Johnson's decision not to run for a second term arrived in a Chicago prepared for war. Mayor Richard Daley, fearing Yippies (antiwar hippies) would spike city reservoirs with the psychedelic drug LSD, had his cops in full riot mode. So for five days, they beat up not only young longhairs but also journalists, even ones on the convention floor.

CHICAGO SUN TIMES

PARKING BY PERMIT ONLY

The Soviet tanks lining a Prague street in August were a harsh reality check for Czechoslovaks. Earlier in the year, their party boss, Alexander Dubček, 46, had bravely talked of nurturing a "socialism with a human face." Those words did not sit well with Moscow. On August 20, Warsaw Pact troops (troops representing the group of allied Eastern European countries dominated by the USSR) numbering 200,000 swept in to snuff out the liberalization movement known as Prague Spring. More than 200,000 were forced to flee the country.

BILL RAY / LIFE

→

TWO V'S FOR VICTORY

His body language was typically awkward, but at an October GOP rally in Ohio, that trademark salute of Richard Nixon's seemed justified. He was pledging "peace with honor" in Vietnam and law and order at home. Further, his opponent, Vice-President Hubert Humphrey, was tarnished by the convention disaster in Chicago. Nixon sensed the prize was his. He was right.

WALTER BENNETT / TIME

MADAM PRIME MINISTER

In 1969, Israel's parliament, the Knesset, selected as the nation's fourth prime minister 70-year-old Golda Meir, shown here with General Haim Bar-Lev. Born in Kiev and raised in Milwaukee (where she was known as Goldie Mabovitch to her public school pupils), Meir had emigrated to Palestine in 1921. Her signature is on Israel's 1948 Proclamation of Independence.

DAVID RUBINGER / TIME

THE RIGHT TO NOT BEAR

In January 1973, in the case *Roe* v. *Wade,* the Supreme Court had held that women may legally obtain an abortion during the first trimester of pregnancy. The ink was barely dry on the High Court's decision when battle lines were drawn. These New Yorkers marched on St. Patrick's Cathedral to protest the Catholic Church's open condemnation of the decision. The battle lines have not changed since.

BETTYE LANE

←

LIGHT MY FIRE

Jimi Hendrix showed. So did Joan Baez. And Carlos Santana. And Grace Slick and the Jefferson Airplane. And Janis Joplin, 26 (inset), with "Bobby McGee." They came in August 1969 to Max Yasgur's farm in Bethel, New York, 60 miles from Woodstock. In renting out his spread, Yasgur, 49, expected "three days of peace and music" — not a circus of the naked and the dead-to-the-world (from drugs). Some 300,000 attended.

JOHN DOMINIS / LIFE

INSET: HENRY DILTZ / CORBIS / BETTMANN

HELTER SKELTER

So read two of the words written in blood at the scene of the savage Beverly Hills murders. The man who ordered them was ex-con and failed songwriter Charles Manson, 35. In August 1969, a "family" of dropouts devoted to him slashed and shot to death five people (including eight-months-pregnant actress Sharon Tate, 26). Why? Manson was angry at a record company exec who often hung out at Tate's estate.

VERNON MERRITT / LIFE

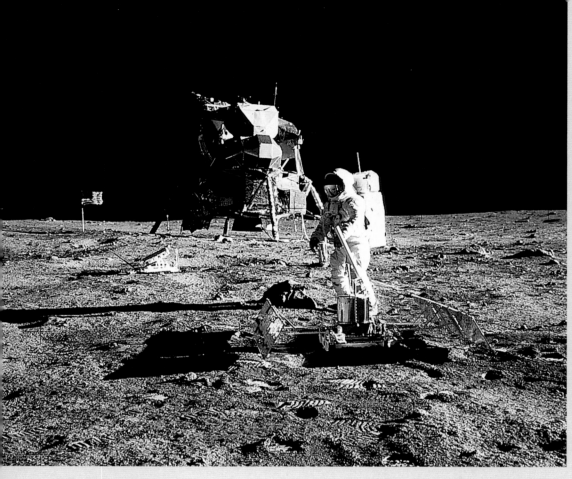

NASA Recycles

The launch of the *Columbia* on April 12, 1981 — and its pilot-controlled landing back at Cape Canaveral 54 hours later — was to have opened a new era of space exploration. With a shuttle fleet that would grow to four, NASA hoped to run a mission a month. But the vehicles needed longer than planned in turnaround time; it took 57 months to send up the first two dozen.

CHARLES TRAINOR / MIAMI NEWS

MISSION: POSSIBLE

On July 20, 1969, just five months short of the target date set eight years earlier by JFK, Neil Armstrong, 38, of Wapakoneta, Ohio, stepped from the *Apollo 11* lander onto the surface of the moon, followed by Buzz Aldrin, 39, of Montclair, New Jersey. Said Armstrong, "That's one small step for man, one giant leap for mankind." Indeed.

NASA

→

THE ORIGINAL RIGHT STUFF

After sifting through 508 applicants for Project Mercury (its accelerated program to send a man into space), the six-month-old National Aeronautics and Space Administration in 1959 announced the chosen seven, whom it called "astronauts." They were, clockwise from top left, Alan Shepard, Gus Grissom, Gordon Cooper, Scott Carpenter, John Glenn, Deke Slayton and Wally Schirra. All would make it off the planet. In 1998, the then four-term senator, Glenn, at 77, repeated the feat and became the oldest person to travel in space.

RALPH MORSE / TIME

Upward Mobility

Sputnik I broke free of the earth before two-thirds of all Americans now alive were born. Perhaps that is why the twinkles in the night sky awe us less than they did our ancestors. Manned missions go unnoted unless their peril is brought tragically home. Unmanned missions? Snore. Yet it is the high-tech drones that have expanded our knowledge of astronomical data. For example, we now know that the universe has expanded since the Big Bang 13 billion years ago, has no boundary and may, or may not, contract. (Probably not.) But all we have learned in a historical eye blink still leaves unanswered the most troubling question: Within the vast heavens beginning where our atmosphere ends, do any other beings dwell?

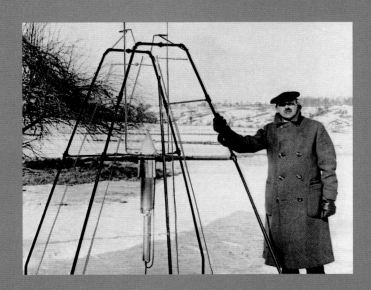

A BABY STEP TOWARD SPACE

He was so sure about his notions for a rocket propulsion system that in 1914, at 32, Robert Goddard filed two patents. A prototype liquid-fueled rocket was eventually built. On March 16, 1926, in Auburn, Massachusetts, Goddard ignited it. The device rose 41 feet into the air. Space was suddenly much closer.

SMITHSONIAN INSTITUTION

175

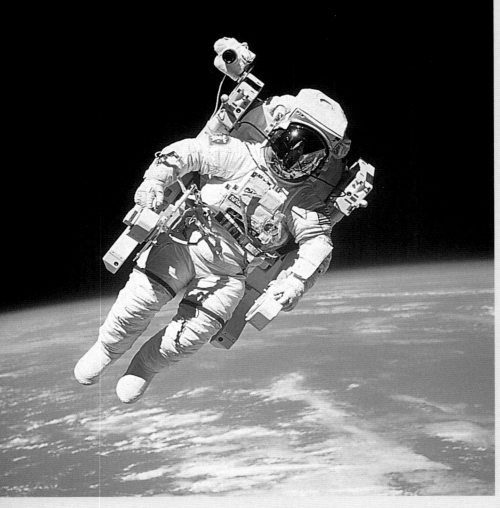

←

FLOATING FREE

On shuttle flight 10, astronauts Bruce McCandless (shown here) and Robert Stewart, using newly developed jet back-packs, became the first to take an untethered (free-floating) spacewalk.

NASA

→

HIGH HANDSHAKE

The space station *Mir* orbited a peaceful 240 miles above a September 1996 storm lashing the Indian Ocean. This photo was taken from NASA's *Atlantis,* which was meeting with the Russian craft to exchange a crew member. It was the fourth binational space hookup since 1975's historic *Apollo-Soyuz* docking.

NASA

SEEING RED

On July 4, 1997, earthlings finally got a ground-level view of the fourth rock from the sun. Earlier landings on Mars, starting with the USSR's *Mars 3* in 1971, were by craft that, unlike NASA's *Pathfinder,* carried no cameras. The 24$\frac{1}{2}$-pound, six-wheeled microrover aboard (top speed: 39 yards per hour) called *Sojourner* beamed back vistas of Ares Vallis, an ancient flood plain, and tested Martian soil, for four months.

NASA

"WE HAVE AN ANOMALY"

January 28, 1986. It was the 25th shuttle mission, and *Challenger*'s 10th flight. Among the crew: Christa McAuliffe, 37, a New Hampshire teacher. Seventy-three seconds after liftoff, a $900 gasket blew. The results were catastrophic. At least four of seven astronauts survived the blast but died when the craft hit the Atlantic Ocean.

MALCOLM DENEMARK / FLORIDA TODAY / LIAISON

FAREWELL

Nixon shrugs his last presidential salute on August 9, 1974.

BILL PIERCE / TIME

A PEACEFUL TRANSITION

On August 9, 1974, Richard Nixon, 61, left the White House via helicopter. Veep Gerald Ford, 61, and his wife, Betty, 56, went back to the White House to wait. Some 90 minutes later, by way of a presigned letter, Nixon became the only U.S. chief executive to resign (to avoid impeachment for his role in the Watergate coverup). At 12:03 P.M., Ford was sworn in as the 38th president. He soon pardoned Nixon; this gesture would cost him the election in 1976.

DENNIS BRACK / BLACK STAR

←

NEARER THE SMOKING GUN

As onetime White House lawyer John Dean faced a Senate panel chaired by Sam Ervin in 1973, a minor 1972 burglary had already become a Washington controversy. The Watergate felons sat in prison. Top Nixon aides had quit. Now Dean, 34, said the President himself was part of the coverup. Then senators learned that Oval Office talks were recorded. Nixon's fight to keep the tapes set off a graver crisis — a constitutional battle that would cost him his office.

GJON MILI / LIFE

BRAINWASHED?

In April 1974, two months after newspaper heiress Patty Hearst, 19, was kidnapped in Berkeley, California, her parents got a snapshot; she had joined her kidnappers, the Symbionese Liberation Army. The SLA robbed banks. Hearst was nabbed 17 months later. A jury rejected her brainwashing defense; she did 22 months before being freed by presidential order.

 →

COMEDY ISN'T PRETTY

ABC had just launched a prime-time hour called *Saturday Night Live with Howard Cosell,* so in October 1975, a rival network called its 90-minute after-hours satirical revue *NBC's Saturday Night* — airing "Live! From New York . . ." The gags were sometimes lame but not the charter troupe: counterclockwise from near right, Chevy Chase, 32; John Belushi, 26; Garrett Morris, 38; Laraine Newman, 23; Jane Curtin, 28; Dan Aykroyd, 23; and Gilda Radner, 29. They're still making us laugh in reruns.

FOTO FANTASIES

LITTLE LEAGUE LEADER

Her 1974 practice swings were for show. Two years earlier, Maria Pepe had pitched three Little League games in Hoboken, New Jersey, before being cut from the team because she wasn't a boy. The state's civil rights office filed a case. The League lost and had to allow girls everywhere to suit up — but by then Maria was 14 and too old to play.

CORBIS / BETTMANN-UPI

ROBERTO CLEMENTE
1934–1972

The great defensive rightfielder turned Pittsburgh's hapless Pirates into contenders and, twice, world champs. Three months after collecting his 3,000th (and last) hit, he flew on a mercy mission to earthquake-torn Nicaragua. The plane crashed. Baseball set aside its five-year-wait rule to make Clemente the first Hall of Famer from Puerto Rico.

AL SATTERWHITE

→
OSKAR SCHINDLER
1908–1974

Known as a Nazi industrialist, he deliberately ran factories at a loss in occupied Poland and Czechoslovakia in order to save Jews (some 1,300 in all) from Hitler's death camps. His efforts led to not only repeated arrests by the Gestapo but also a brief postwar detention by the Allies. Schindler's story was popularized by Steven Spielberg's 1993 epic movie, *Schindler's List.* Schindler rests in Israel, where he is revered as a Righteous Gentile.

PHOTOGRAPHER UNKNOWN

→
WOODY GUTHRIE
1912–1967

Saloons and hobo camps were favorite haunts of the one-man protest band (and hero for Sixties folksingers like son Arlo and Bob Dylan). Of his 1,000-plus songs, the best known is "This Land Is Your Land." It was later used in upbeat advertising campaigns. Funny; Woody wrote it to condemn the ownership of private property.

ERIC SCHAAL / LIFE

ERNESTO (CHE) GUEVARA
1928–1967

An Argentine of Spanish and Irish descent (one grandmother was a U.S. citizen), he gave up a medical career to foster revolution in five countries. He authored two books on guerilla warfare. In 1956, Guevara hooked up with Fidel Castro; Cuba was to be his only winner. His last guerrilla campaign was in Bolivia. The CIA found him, the Bolivians shot him.

LEE LOCKWOOD / TIME INC.

→
EARL WARREN
1891–1974

As California's attorney general in 1942, Warren urged that the state's Japanese-Americans be sent to camps. But as Supreme Court Chief Justice, he usually championed the rights of minorities. The Warren Court outlawed racial segregation in public schools in 1954 (*Brown* v. *Board of Education*) and in 1966 (*Miranda* v. *Arizona*) ruled that suspects must be read their constitutional rights before police questioning.

PAUL S. CONKLIN / TIME INC.

REQUIEM

J. R. R. TOLKIEN
1892–1973

Inspired by the medieval literature he taught, the Oxford gentleman began writing tales of a gnarly realm called Middle Earth that was populated by hobbits, dwarves and elves. *The Hobbit* was published in 1937. Tolkien finished his epic sequel, *The Lord of the Rings*, in 1955. Thus, the 1,191-page trilogy was available in paperback by the time hippies were ready to tune in.

SNOWDON / TRANSWORLD CAMERA PRESS

A GLOBAL BURST OF FREEDOM

1976–1992

On its 200th birthday, the United States of America numbered 50 (from 13 original states), and its 218 million citizens (from 2.5 million) spoke 350-plus languages (from a handful).

J. P. LAFFONT / SYGMA

LIBERTY FOR ALL

by Gary Paulsen

It can of course be argued that there have been many outbursts of liberty in our history. Certainly America's declaration in 1776 that it would be independent from England, and the subsequent convincing of France to help, which in turn broke France financially and led to its own revolution against its government for freedom from monarchy, would qualify.

Or even the 1215 signing of the Magna Carta charter, which stipulated the basis for laws that still govern us — the very concept that people have rights — was definitely the beginning of such an explosion. And yet . . .

There was something about the period between 1976 and 1992 that sets it apart, or perhaps more accurately, several things that make it a unique time in history. When viewed from a whole world perspective, this was the most volatile period since World War II.

Consider: The Berlin wall came down. The Soviet Union began to collapse and with it came an end to the Cold War — a nightmare of implied world destruction that had lasted decades — which allowed expressions of freedom that had been denied a whole generation. Soweto, the black township in South Africa, exploded in riots when police shot and killed children who were peacefully demonstrating for new schools, and the world at last saw, and began to change, the ugly face of apartheid, which had kept the blacks in South Africa in little more than slavery. The war in Vietnam with its attendant horrors had just ended, and the war in Afghanistan, which would become known as Russia's Vietnam, was just starting. Elvis Presley died in 1977 of a drug overdose (and John Lennon of the Beatles was murdered three years later). Princess Diana, an unknown teenager, married Prince Charles in 1981, only to die tragically in a car crash after becoming one of the world's most famous celebrities. Conservative Margaret Thatcher became the first woman prime minister of England. *Thriller* by Michael Jackson became the number one LP of all time while the film *Star Wars* dominated the film industry and

AN OOLONG, I BELIEVE?

Campaigning American politicians taste whatever the locals offer. In 1979 British by-elections, Margaret Thatcher tasted tea. And passed the test. Returned to Parliament at 54, she was named her nation's first woman prime minister. It was a position that the iron-willed Thatcher (one nickname: Attila the Hen) would hold for 11 years, a 20th Century record.

BEN MARTIN / TIME

made special effects the buzzword in the movie industry from then on. AIDS came into our consciousness, and the public's understanding was helped a great deal by the courage of Rock Hudson, the famous film star who admitted he had the disease. In sports, gymnast Nadia Comaneci scored a perfect 10 while Martina Navratilova retired with 167 tennis titles, the most of *any* player in history. The *Challenger* space

vehicle exploded. The world, or a large part of it, went to war in Kuwait when Saddam Hussein invaded.

All these occurrences stand alone, and each has its point in history, as all historical events do, but what makes them unique and at the same time brings them all together is the immediacy of the event.

Before the American Civil War almost nobody but combat soldiers knew what war was really like, how truly horrible it was, how explosively violent. Then Matthew Brady and his team of photographers took pictures of battlefield casualties, in all their horror, and published them. For the first time in history, the general public became aware of the truth. There was an immediate outcry from

WE GIVE IT A 10

She would land perfectly on the balance beam at the 1976 Olympics. The 14-year-old, 86-pound gymnast Nadia Comaneci won this and two other golds at Montreal (notching the first seven perfect scores in Games history). But her brutal training in Communist Romania had taken a toll; the next year, she attempted suicide. Comaneci defected to America in 1989.

CO RENTMEESTER

wives and mothers of men in the Army, a demand (that was heeded) for generals and other officers to pay more attention to their jobs and not waste so many men with poor judgment and tactics.

That concept of the immediacy of the event has been drastically, radically accelerated in mod-ern times. When Rodney King was beaten by the Los Angeles police in March of 1991, it was video-taped by a bystander who gave the tape to a news station, and literally within hours the world knew of the beating; when the police were subsequently acquitted of the beating, Los Angeles erupted in riots, with 50 dead and more than 2,000 injured.

When Madonna sang "Like a Virgin" or took her clothes off or when Dr. Seuss (Theodor Geisel) passed away, we knew of it at once.

It is perhaps the greatest phenomenon of our modern age, this immediacy of knowledge. For better or worse, people have tried to control it,

keep it from happening; during the Gulf War the government and military went to tremendous lengths to keep the general press from knowing what was happening, even at times lying to them and using them to unwittingly give misinformation to the enemy. But it really wasn't effective.

People are intensely curious and feel the need to know everything that is happening to them, and to their world, and technology has advanced far enough to allow them to have that knowledge. There has always been history, always been joy or tragedy, but now — starting in the Seventies and coming right through to the present — now we can *know* what is happening.

Gary Paulsen is a three-time Newbery Honor winner for The Winter Room, Dogsong *and* Hatchet, *which also won the Dorothy Canfield Fisher Award. Mr. Paulsen was awarded the Margaret A. Edwards Award honoring his lifetime contribution in writing books for young adults. His many other books include* Woodsong, The Crossing, Canyons *and* Dancing Carl.

BLONDE AMBITION

Her signature song is, of course, "Like a Virgin." No pop star in the 1980s or since has been more skilled at reinventing herself than Madonna (Ciccone, above, 26, at a 1985 concert). Whether a boy toy or a material girl, this blonde knew how to have fun and make money, too. In 1992, she signed a deal with Time Warner to create her own record, publishing and motion picture company.

ANTHONY SUAU / LIAISON

IN A GALAXY FAR, FAR AWAY

O.K., so the desert was actually Tunisia, not on the planet Tatooine. And those droids were actually British actors Anthony Daniels, 30 (left as C-3PO), and Kenny Baker, 41 (as R2-D2). Still, we suspended disbelief over 1977's *Star Wars,* filmed by director George Lucas, 33, for $7.8 million. *The Phantom Menace,* the fourth episode (a total of nine are planned) of the saga that changed not only Hollywood but also pop culture, was released in 1999 and set a record first-day take of more than $28 million.

LUCASFILM

A HISTORIC HUG

Five years earlier, there was only enmity between Egyptian president Anwar Sadat, 59 (left), and Israeli prime minister Menachem Begin, 65; now, in September 1978, they were in open embrace. The Yom Kippur War had cost both nations dearly. So after 12 grueling days of talks at Camp David refereed by President Jimmy Carter, 54, Sadat and Begin unveiled the first Israeli-Arab peace accord ever.

DAVID HUME KENNERLY

 →

BURDEN OF GRIEF

Young Hector Petersen was peacefully protesting the bad schools in South Africa's black township of Soweto when he was shot dead (with three others) by riot police. The June 1976 incident sparked an uprising that claimed some 1,000 more lives in the next 18 months. One who died, though not in Soweto but under detention: 30-year-old activist Steven Biko.

AP

LAMBS TO SLAUGHTER

A year after following cult leader Jim Jones to equatorial Guyana, members of his People's Temple were fatally betrayed by him. Jones, 47, who had fled the San Francisco Bay Area because his tactics were being investigated, panicked on November 18, 1978, when congressional investigators arrived. He had some of them shot. Then he told his flock to drink poisoned Fla-Vor-Aid. After some 900 had, he put a gun to his own head.

DAVID HUME KENNERLY

TEST-TUBE TODDLER

Fifteen-month-old Louise Brown of England was a September 1979 guest on Phil Donahue's popular talk show. Her claim to fame? She was the first child born of an egg fertilized outside her mother (who could not conceive but did carry the then implanted in vitro, or test-tube, baby to term). Louise didn't need biochemist Pierre Soupart to attest to her obvious good health.

CORBIS / BETTMANN-UPI

WORKERS OF THE WORLD UNITE

One aspect of communism had always troubled Polish shipyard electrician Lech Walesa: In urging workers of the world to unite, it also banned them from uniting in unions. In 1979, at 36, he founded, at his workplace in Gdansk, Poland, a movement called Solidarity. Walesa placed himself in personal jeopardy, but both he and the movement survived to fight for the rights of workers and send shock waves through the entire Soviet empire.

AP / WIDE WORLD

TRASHING A LEADER (AND SOME INFIDELS)

No one was more stunned in January 1979 than the Shah Mohammad Reza Pahlavi of Iran. After 37 years, the westernized Shah, 59, was told rather pointedly by conservative Muslims, called Shiites, to quit the Peacock Throne. Two weeks later, adoring Shiites welcomed their Ayatollah Ruhollah Khomeini, 79, back from a 15-year exile. In October, Jimmy Carter allowed the Shah to enter the U.S. for treatment of his terminal cancer. Khomeini got even by allowing young fundamentalist radicals to seize the American embassy in Iran and 52 hostages (below). The 444-day siege cost Carter reelection in 1980.

LEFT: KAVEH GOLESTAN

BELOW: ALAIN MINAM / LIAISON

ACTIONS AND REACTIONS

These Afghan guerrillas didn't care that the Soviet paratroopers landing in Kabul in late 1979 had been invited by a government that claimed to be in power but wasn't. The mujahedin wanted them (and the 100,000 Soviet soldiers who followed) out. So did the Muslim states supporting the rebels with arms and cash. So did the CIA, which even flew in a passionate blind cleric from Egypt to advise the mujahedin. After the humbled Soviets withdrew in 1989, the cleric, Sheikh Omar Abdul Rahman, was allowed secret entry to the U.S. He would soon repay the U.S. by masterminding the bombing of the World Trade Center.

STEVE MCCURRY / MAGNUM

→

MAGIC AND THE LEGEND

Larry Bird, 22, had shown that white men need not jump in leading Indiana State (11,474 students) to the 1979 NCAA finals. Waiting were Earvin (Magic) Johnson, 19, and overdog Michigan State (44,756 students). David didn't beat Goliath. But the two All-Americans ignited March Madness by putting on a show they then took to the NBA.

JAMES DRAKE / SPORTS ILLUSTRATED

MY FELLOW AMERICANS

FDR was the first president to harness modern mass communications when, from the White House on March 12, 1933, he addressed the nation live on radio. Roosevelt conducted 29 more "fireside chats" (including this one in 1941 in front of Latin American diplomats) during the remainder of his years in office.

THOMAS D. MCAVOY / LIFE

WATCHING A WAR BEGIN

The images Americans saw on the night of January 16, 1991, seemed like an early low-resolution video-arcade game: rising sheets of antiaircraft fire, sudden flares of detonating bombs. It was not Missile Command but rather the first Allied air raids on Baghdad. Operation Desert Storm had started on live TV.

CNN

HERE COMES THE BRIDE

In 1969, some 200 million people worldwide tuned in for the formal presentation, at Caernarvon, of the Prince of Wales. On July 29, 1981, the audience swelled to 750 million for the marriage, at Westminster Abbey in London, of Prince Charles, 32, to Lady Diana Frances Spencer, 20.

DAVID BURNETT / CONTACT

LIVE FROM ATLANTA

At 6 P.M. Eastern time on June 1, 1980, any of America's 15.2 million cable-TV subscribers surfing their channels might have seen Atlanta-based entrepreneur Ted Turner, then 41, personally inaugurate his Cable News Network, or CNN. A loser, said skeptics; there wasn't enough news to fill out a 24-hour schedule. Soon to follow: 24-hour networks for music, finance and sports.

DAVID BURNETT / CONTACT

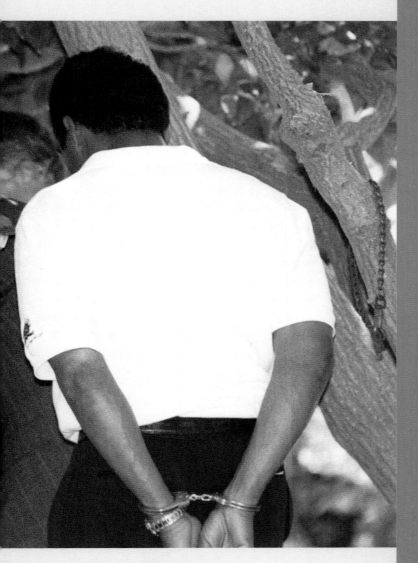

IF THE GLOVE DOESN'T FIT

On June 13, 1994, 12 hours after a double homicide in Brentwood, California, one victim's ex was held for questioning. A few days later, the former football star O. J. Simpson, 47, was charged with two counts of homicide and then became a fugitive. He drove his friend's Bronco down I-405 with police in pursuit and news choppers broadcasting live from the scene. The next year's televised trial turned into a three-ring judicial circus starring lawyers, witnesses and even the judge. The evidence trickling out over 36 weeks convinced jurors that yes, they must acquit.

JOHN BARR / LIAISON

See It Now

In 490 B.C., it is told, one man ran 25-plus miles to tell fellow Athenians of their victory at Marathon. Information traveled no faster than the swiftest messenger. The American colonies declared independence on July 4, 1776, but King George III didn't hear the news until mid-August. In 1861, it took 10 days and teams of horseback riders to relay the news between Missouri and California — but the Pony Express was surpassed 18 months later by the first transcontinental telegraph. Radio cut everyone in on the electronic action, and today, the latest from anywhere is but a mouse-click away. Round-the-clock, round-the-world information has a downside, however. If we let our reflexes respond, we sacrifice the time to verify, to reflect, to frame options. The upside is knowledge, which empowers. Why else do dictators try to limit such messengers as satellite TV?

EXTRA! EXTRA!

Telegraphers quickly sped news of the British victory in May 1902 across the 6,000 miles separating South Africa and England, but then it was up to newsboys to spread the word around London. One British journalist who made a name for himself covering the Boer War: future prime minister Winston Churchill.

TIME INC.

TARGET: THE PRESIDENT

By waving to the crowd as he departed from a luncheon at a D.C. hotel on March 30, 1981, Ronald Reagan, 70, left himself open to a .22 bullet. The aspiring assassin, hoping to catch the eye of Jodie Foster, an actress he was obsessed with, also wounded three others, most critically press secretary Jim Brady, 40, who was confined to a wheelchair for the rest of his life. Reagan's recovery began in the OR: Eyeing the docs, he quipped, "Please tell me you're Republicans."

RON EDMONDS / AP

TARGET: THE POPE

In greeting the 10,000 worshipers at his weekly audience in St. Peter's Square on May 13, 1981, Pope John Paul II, 60, left himself open to two 9mm bullets to the abdomen. The would-be assassin was an escaped Turkish con who said his motives were not religious. He claimed to be a hired gun for Bulgarians fronting for Moscow, which feared the Polish-born pontiff would lend moral aid to Lech Walesa's Solidarity movement.

FOTAM

FUTURE MILLIONAIRES

Computer novices Paul G. Allen, 27 (left, in July 1981), and William H. Gates III, 25, had heard that IBM, about to market its first personal computer, needed some nuts-and-bolts system code. The Seattle pals pooled $50,000 to buy an existing piece of software that they tweaked and retitled MicroSoft Disk Operating System (MS-DOS). IBM gave the kids a break and licensed it. Little did IBM guess that the two would found Microsoft, America's current leading software company, which, by 1996, had more than 20,000 employees and $8.7 billion in revenue. In 1999, *Forbes* magazine listed Bill Gates as the richest person in the world for the fifth year in a row.

SEATTLE POST-INTELLIGENCER

WHAT RIGHT TO VOTE?

By 1982, El Salvadorans had understandably come to fear Election Day violence. (Here, troops in suburban San Salvador clean the streets of dead leftists.) The Central American nation of 4.6 million was for 12 years a free-fire zone in which Cuban-backed guerrillas and U.S.-backed death squads clashed; a truce was reached in 1992.

DON MCCULLIN

PAGING DR. HUXTABLE

The first black to co-star in a prime-time drama (1965's *I Spy*) struck out on his next three series. But in 1984, Bill Cosby, 47 (here with Keshia Knight Pulliam, five), tried a new sitcom on NBC. Cosby played an obstetrician and father of five. *The Cosby Show* would finish in the top five each of its first seven seasons (including at No. 1 from 1985 to 1990) and thus command record rerun fees (half a billion dollars for 125 episodes).

NBC

I'M NOT LIKE OTHER GUYS

Thriller was rock's Main Event in 1983 and won a record seven Grammy Awards. The LP by Michael Jackson, 25, is No. 1 all-time (25 million and counting) and the unusually long video legitimized the new cable service MTV. Sadly, the onetime Jackson Five cutie wasn't the Mike to be like. From moonwalker extraordinaire, he morphed into a morbid collector (bidding on Elephant Man's bones) and then a cosmetic-surgery-ravaged hermit.

VESTRON VIDEO

E.T. PHONE BANKER

The little critter (with on-planet pal Henry Thomas, 10) required more high-tech wizardry from director Steven Spielberg than did Bruce, his Great White. But then 1982's *E.T. The Extra-Terrestrial* had more box-office teeth ($400 million versus *Jaws*'s $260 million) and so much charm that it drew a PG despite a little coarse language.

UNIVERSAL STUDIOS

QUEEN OF THE TALK SHOWS

Oprah Winfrey's boots were made for talkin'. At 31, the onetime TV news-reader was hosting an A.M. show in Chicago; in 1986, she went national. Oprah's emotive, confessional style (childhood abuse, weight issues) fast made her the queen of syndication. On buying rights to her show in 1988, Winfrey also became TV's most powerful, not to mention richest, woman.

KEVIN HORAN

LISTEN UP, HOMEY

The sample-scratching, insult-woofing music that started in America's inner cities stayed there until 1984, when the LP *Run-D.M.C.* went gold. The artists, from near right: Jason Mizell, 19; Joseph (Run) Simmons, 19; and Darryl (D.M.C.) McDaniels, 20. The group got a bigger boost when their "Rock Box" became MTV's first rap video.

KEN REGAN / CAMERA 5

Take It Out of Petty Cash

When Michael Milken talked, Wall Street listened; at 40, he was the king of junk bonds. Entrepreneurs used the high-risk, high-yield paper to fund start-ups (like MCI) or fund hostile takeovers (RJR Nabisco). In 1990, Milken admitted he played favorites. He had to do hard time, agree to a lifetime ban on trading securities, and pay a $600 million fine. Still, that was merely $50 million more than his salary and bonus for 1987.

Steve Smith

A Hole in the Sky

The pink area in this computer-tinted satellite photo was not pretty to atmospheric researchers: It confirmed that the ozone layer over Antarctica was thinning. Not until 1958 did scientists study the atmospheric layer (five to 25 miles up) that absorbs harmful ultraviolet rays. It thickened until 1970, then began to thin, increasing the risk of skin cancer. Whether the thinning is permanent or a cyclical phenomenon (like El Niño) remains unclear.

NASA

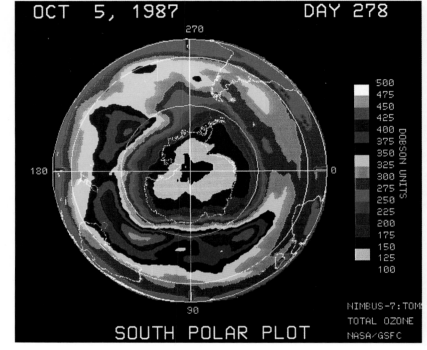

Bad News, Good News

Nature designed an otter's fur to repel sea-water, but this otter was in Prince William Sound, Alaska, in 1989, after the tanker *Exxon Valdez* ran aground. The tanker leaked some 11 million gallons of oil, coating 1,300 miles of Alaska's shoreline. Wildlife beyond count died, some colonies forever. Yet predictions of long-term disaster over-looked the fact that the Sound had recouped from another major ecodisaster: the earth-quake of 1964.

Tony Dawson

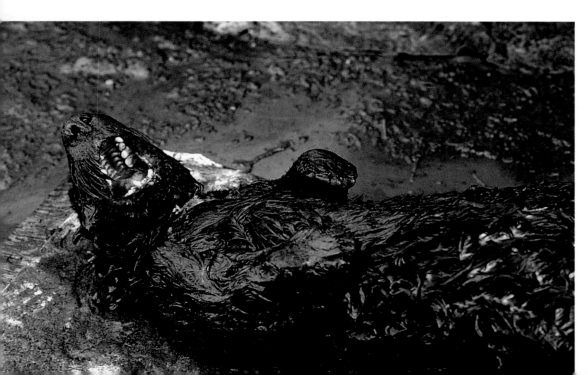

MAN OF STEELY NERVES

An unforgettable image from 1989: one lone Chinese against a column of T-59 tanks in central Beijing. Even more astonishing was his climbing onto the tank and chatting through the hatch with the crew. Cordiality soon vanished. China's rulers wanted 100-acre Tiananmen Square cleared of a pro-democracy sit-in that began in mid-April. On June 4, the army went in. No body count has ever been released.

STUART FRANKLIN / MAGNUM

A LOPSIDED DUEL IN THE DESERT

The fastest route home was also the deadliest for Iraqis whose occupation of Kuwait abruptly ended in late February 1991. Saddam Hussein, their self-venerating president, had made the mother of all miscalculations. His country and its tiny neighbor (population: 1.9 million, only half native Kuwaitis) had long argued over a shared oil field. Already praised by the U.S. for his war with Iran, Hussein in mid-1990 got official word that Washington didn't care about Persian Gulf border disputes. He promptly seized Kuwait. Whereupon 28 nations (nine of them Arab states) formed a 690,000-strong force led by U.S. general Norman Schwarzkopf, 56 (inset). Operation Desert Storm opened with fierce air and missile attacks on Iraq. More than sixty thousand bombing runs were flown in all. On February 23, the ground campaign began. It took 100 hours to clear Kuwait of Iraqis. But the drive stopped short of Baghdad, leaving Hussein, 53, still in dictatorial power.

DENNIS BRACK / BLACK STAR

INSET: HARRY BENSON

THE END OF THE USSR

On May 29, 1990, Boris Yeltsin, 59, became president of Russia — and thus No. 2 man to Mikhail Gorbachev in a USSR on life support. Its Eastern European empire was gone, and member republics were seceding. In August 1991, Kremlin diehards tried a coup. Yeltsin heroically intervened; then, after parliament shuttered the Communist Party, he got Gorbachev to dissolve the Soviet Union itself. After much speculation about his failing health and a seemingly weakened position of political power, Yeltsin resigned from office on New Year's Eve 1999.

AP

→

A FUNNY THING . . .

. . . happened on the way to Election Day, 1992: Ross Perot, 62 (and, as ever, on *Larry King Live*). The Texas data-processing tycoon, mad at George Bush over Vietnam MIAs, checkbooked himself into the race and took on the president. The U.S. economy soured. The Rodney King case verdicts rocked Los Angeles. More of Perot's 19.7 million votes came from discontented Republicans than from Democrats.

SHELLY KATZ / LIAISON

CAUGHT ON TAPE

It was a case of same song, different verse in Los Angeles in 1991. Early on March 3, cops were right to bust the driver who had led them on a high-speed chase — but not with their nightsticks, boots and stun guns. An onlooker videotaped the attack and gave his sickening footage to a local TV station. In days, the brutalized victim, Rodney King, a 25-year-old laborer, became the symbol of the LAPD's insensitive treatment of minorities. Four white officers were put on trial. Their acquittal a year later, by an all-white suburban jury, inflamed the city's heavily black South-Central district. The riot ran for two days. Its toll: 50-plus dead, 2,000-plus injured, 12,000 arrested, $1 billion in damages and a racial divide that would soon become evident in the murder trial of O. J. Simpson.

SCOTT WEERSING / LIAISON

→

OUT OF THE OZARKS

The Bush Administration was still basking in Desert Storm's patriotic glow when from the mosh pit of 1992 Democratic long shots and no-names rose Bill Clinton. Hadn't the Arkansas governor, 45, already fessed up in prime time to a less than perfect marriage? Clinton went on to win two presidential terms but was impeached by the U.S. House of Representatives. He was subsequently acquitted in the impeachment trial in the U.S. Senate.

CYNTHIA JOHNSON / TIME

GEORGIA O'KEEFFE
1887–1986

Her earliest works were abstracts, but by the time other American painters embraced the school, she had moved on to her signature series of over-size flowers. O'Keeffe resettled in New Mexico in the 1940s. There, her startlingly sensual vision turned grave and haunting: The late canvases are often of sun-bleached skulls in the desert.

DAVID GAHR

BOB MARLEY
1945–1981

When "I Shot the Sheriff" was covered by a Brit (Eric Clapton), the curious sought out the artist whose song it was. By then, of course, Marley was already a legend in his native Jamaica. His Rastafarian dreadlocks and enjoyment of *ganja,* a slang term for marijuana, played as well off-island as his reggae. Also a political activist, he survived a 1976 assault but not cancer.

RICHARD CREAMER / RETNA, LTD.

JOHN LENNON
1940–1980

The newly cut "(Just Like) Starting Over" would be his 58th chart hit, including those with the Beatles. The psychic wounds from the Fab Four's breakup were healing. His exbandmates were doing well. There was even rumor of a reunion concert. But on December 8, a failed songwriter turned stalker shot 40-year-old Lennon dead outside his Manhattan apartment building.

DIEGO GOLDBERG / SYGMA

REQUIEM

DR. SEUSS
1904–1991

Theodor Geisel, known to many as Dr. Seuss, won honors for writing ads and World War II documentaries. Then he won fame and fortune for writing (and illustrating) 47 books for children of all ages. A few of his most beloved, tonguetwisting books are *The Cat in the Hat, How the Grinch Stole Christmas* (both 1957) and *Green Eggs and Ham* (1960).

JOHN BRYSON

←

TENNESSEE WILLIAMS
1911–1983

He loaded his dramas with faded belles, cripples and brutes from the Deep South, but their tortured search for happiness and forgiveness is universal. In just 11 years, Williams (born in Mississippi) wrote *The Glass Menagerie, A Streetcar Named Desire* and *Cat on a Hot Tin Roof.* Booze and drugs were his downfall; he choked to death on a medicine-bottle cap.

W. EUGENE SMITH / LIFE

→

JIM HENSON
1936–1990

Big Bird, Cookie Monster and the grouchy Oscar belonged to *Sesame Street,* the PBS show that the innovative puppetmeister helped make must-watch kid TV. But the Muppets belonged to Henson, who built them into a showbiz empire. Kermit, Miss Piggy and dozens of others starred in a weekly show (broadcast in 100 countries) along with an array of famous human stars; the Muppets even starred in their own feature films. Until his death (from a rare but treatable bacterial infection), Henson always found time to give voice to his alter ego, the gentle, wry Kermit T. Frog.

JIM HENSON COMPANY

MARGARET MEAD
1901–1978

Mead began her anthropological career at age eight by studying her sisters' speech. In the mid-1920s, she lived with natives on Samoa and New Guinea; they inspired her revolutionary thesis that sex roles are determined by culture. Mead's lack of supporting data invited criticism, but not her zest for fieldwork.

CORBIS / BETTMANN

ALFRED HITCHCOCK
1899–1980

Hitchcock framed his psychologically complex and technically innovative thrillers as races against the clock. He dragged out suspense like a gleeful psycho. He gave his heroes flaws not unlike his own, which emerged from a youth colored by vertigo, a condition in which a person's surroundings seem to whirl about. Among his most memorable films are *Rear Window* (1954), *Psycho* (1960) and *The Birds* (1963). He treated actors like cattle, yet prodded, from some, career performances. But it was his trademark brief acting appearances that made each of his 53 movies a Hitchcock.

LISA LARSEN / LIFE

OURFUTURE.COM

1993–1999

There was no silencing this lamb's creation in July 1996. Dolly, here on her first birthday, was from neither the union of ram and ewe nor a test tube; she was cloned by Scottish geneticist Ian Wilmut from a single cell of her mother.

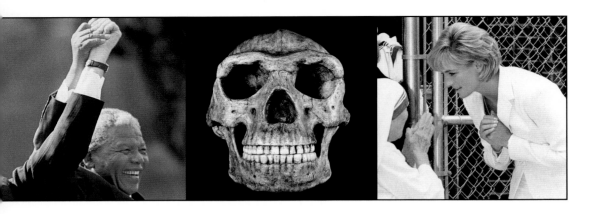

GOOD WINS OUT

by Cynthia Rylant

In 1993, my son and I moved across country from Ohio to Oregon. If we'd been pioneers in covered wagons, we'd have said good-bye to all our old friends in Ohio *forever*, for we'd almost surely never see them or even hear from them again. Once across the country in a bumpy covered wagon is usually enough for anybody.

But we didn't cross in a covered wagon, we crossed in a *station wagon* (a white Volvo with two dogs sleeping in the back). We also didn't have to say good-bye to old friends forever. Because we had the post office, FedEx, UPS, AT&T, MCI, Sprint and the Internet. We could also just fly back in a jiffy if we wanted to.

We were living in a techno-age. Computers were everywhere. And, for the most part, they were doing very good things, like keeping old friends together.

Computers also, in these last years of the century, were changing many of the old myths we'd come to live by. Some of these changes really caught the world by surprise.

For example, now people don't actually have to meet face-to-face anymore to become friends or to fall in love. Now they do it on the Internet, at three in the morning, sometimes 10,000 miles apart.

Another change is privacy. A lot of privacy is being lost. People find out all about one another on the Internet: where they live, what they buy, how much money they have, what diseases they carry. Some people set up video cameras in their rooms and broadcast their private lives to the world all day and all night. Instead of keeping scrapbooks, some people build their own Web pages and "paste" in them their favorite photos, lists of their favorite foods, their "Best Time Ever" and their "Worst Time Ever."

And parents now must teach their children that bad people aren't just down dark alleys anymore. The Internet can be as full of danger as the woods Little Red Riding Hood had to walk into.

On the other hand, it can also be a place full of goodness, of love and support between people who meet on the Web and find out that they are very much alike. People feel less alone. Outcasts feel less cast out. The Internet gives those who can find no soul mates at home or at school or at work another place to search: the world.

It is a techno-age. And technology is still very new to human beings who have been digging around in the dirt for centuries and centuries. It still feels a little scary.

So it is no wonder that when, in the late 1990s, some children and teenagers brought guns to school to kill as many other children and teenagers as they could before their bullets ran out, a lot of people blamed technology. They

Gone Postal

In this tiny Montana shack he built mail bombs — 16 in 17 years — that killed three, maimed 23. Because his targets were associated with universities and airlines, federal agents nicknamed him the Unabomber. The Unabomber explained his technophobic rationale in a published 1995 manifesto. His kid brother recognized the author's style. In 1998, Ted Kaczynski, 55, drew life times four.

RICHARD BARNES

Teenagers with Guns

On a hilltop in Littleton, Colorado, stood crosses for the 15 victims of an April 1999 high school massacre. Included were two for the young shooters (one at far right), who wounded 23 before shooting themselves. The pro-gun NRA lamented this, as well as seven earlier student rampages that killed 17, but then opened its convention in nearby Denver anyway.

KEVIN MOLONEY / LIAISON

blamed computers and computer games, they blamed TVs and television shows, they blamed stereos and rock CDs.

If it seems that all at once your world is sick, you naturally look around to find the bug that caused the illness. In these times, the bug most often blamed is usually the one crawling around inside a piece of technology.

But the mysteries of kindness and cruelty, of faith and despair, of trust and fear are much too deep and too complex to be explained away by pointing a finger at a popular song or a popular game or a Sunday night television show.

We'll have to do better than that.

Perhaps more can be learned from looking at the best of human accomplishment rather than at

BURNING BRIGHT

On April 13, 1997, Tiger Woods, 21 (here, accepting his Masters jacket from outgoing champ Nick Faldo), became the first African-Asian-American to take one of golf's major titles. He didn't just win the tournament. He recorded the lowest Masters score ever and the highest margin of victory in a major since the 1862 British Open. The Augusta course where he won was, until 1975, closed to people of color unless they were caddies. On tour, Woods would still occasionally hear racist remarks not aimed at the Thai portion of his heritage.

JOHN BIEVER / SPORTS ILLUSTRATED

the worst. In the last years of the century, some remarkable people taught us all how to live with grace and courage.

Lance Armstrong won the Tour de France — a 2,500-mile bike race — only two and a half years after being diagnosed with cancer. Some might have given up. He just decided not to.

Tiger Woods, a man of both youth and color, won the Masters golf championship although some believed he was both the wrong age and the wrong race to do it. He chose to ignore them.

Even Chelsea Clinton, the young daughter of our controversial president, taught everyone in this country how to carry on during painful times with bravery, graciousness and compassion. It is not uncommon that a child seems far wiser than the parent.

In the arts and popular culture, young people found many expressions of who they were and what they believed in the 1990s. Rap music continued to reflect their passion, their anger, their higher ideals in a world they found less and less idyllic.

There were television shows like *The Simpsons*, hilariously portraying a far from perfect cartoon family who, in an oddly heartwarming way, managed to completely screw everything up.

Children — and adults — of the Nineties needed all the comic relief they could find when it came to families. Not for a long time had most families looked like the 1950s model: Mom in apron, Dad at work, children with crisply ironed clothes and no anxiety.

But both religious leaders and politicians chastised the country for its failed "family values," wagging fingers at single-parent homes, mixed-race marriages and same-sex couples.

People were making their own definitions of what *family* meant, and this did not sit well with those who had fundamental views of right and wrong.

But in spite of the wagging fingers, the country seemed to be, on the whole, both good and optimistic. An interest in angels surged, and kind and winged spirits could be seen everywhere — on television, in books and movies. *Star Wars Episode I: The Phantom Menace* appeared in theaters in 1999, and fans lined up for blocks for a chance to rally once more against the Dark Side.

And as the end of the century, and of the millennium, approached, this optimism that Good would win out overpowered the dark predictions of apocalypse and destruction and the end of the world. Even the computers fooled everybody and kept working.

Children read Harry Potter and dreamed of making wonderful things happen.

In the next century, they probably will.

Cynthia Rylant is the author of the Newbery Award–winning Missing May *and* A Fine White Dust, *a Newbery Honor title. Her picture book* When I Was Young in the Mountains, *illustrated by Diane Goode, received the American Book Award and also won a Caldecott Honor. Ms. Rylant has written more than 70 books for children, including* Boston Globe-Horn Book *Award winner* Appalachia: The Voices of Sleeping Birds *and the Poppleton books.*

AN EARLY ENCOUNTER

On the White House rope line in summer 1995 was West Wing intern Monica Lewinsky, 22. What took place between her and Bill Clinton is graphically documented in independent counsel Kenneth Starr's 1998 report, whose juicy parts made it sell like hotcakes. In 1999, after the President survived impeachment, a quicky biography of Monica hit bookstores. It didn't sell as well.

SYGMA

RUSH-HOUR TERROR

At rush hour in Tokyo on March 20, 1995, 12 subway riders were killed and 3,800 felled by the nerve gas sarin. The perpetrators: a cult called Aum Shinrikyo led by Shoko Asahara, 40. It could have been worse. Asahara is on a shortlist of terrorists thought to be after a sample of smallpox virus, for which there is no longer an adequate supply of vaccine.

ASAHI SHIMBUN

DANGEROUS PEACE

Israeli prime minister Yitzhak Rabin, 71, did not hide his feelings at a 1993 photo op with Bill Clinton and PLO leader Yasir Arafat, 64. But he then shook hands on an accord to give Palestinians more autonomy. The next year, he signed a peace pact with Jordan. Thirteen months later, in Tel Aviv, Rabin was shot dead by a right-wing Israeli.

CYNTHIA JOHNSON / TIME

←

TALL TARGETS

Had the terrorist parked his rental truck closer to a girder in the garage below Manhattan's World Trade Center in February 1993, the blast would have killed far more than six and injured far more than 1,000. The hit was directed by Omar Abdul Rahman, 54, ex-adviser to Afghanistan's mujahedin (see page 194). The blind cleric hoped to topple one 110-story tower into its twin.

MARK CARDWELL / REUTERS / ARCHIVE PHOTOS

→

BETRAYED BY BLOODLINES

Some 1.5 million fled the African nation of Rwanda in spring 1994 — this family to next-door Tanzania — when five centuries of tribal hostility between Hutus and Tutsis flared into another civil war. An estimated 500,000 were less fortunate: They died so brutally that in 1998, a U.N. tribunal found the nation's then prime minister guilty of genocide.

ALEXANDER JOE / AFP

WHERE THERE'S SMOKE

In April 1994, eight corporate tobacco chiefs swore to Congress that they were not merchants of evil. Though their mainstay product had been declared hazardous to humans by the U.S. Surgeon General 30 years earlier, the cigarette moguls insisted they had no personal knowledge of health risks. Yet in 1997, their industry headed off a legion of lawsuits by coughing up $368.5 billion.

JOHN DURICKA / AP

GLORY IS FLEETING

Newt Gingrich's prize for steering the GOP to congressional majorities in 1994: the House Speakership (and a *Time* Man of the Year cover the next year, here being photographed by Gregory Heisler). The ex-history teacher, 52, had correctly read the backlash against big-government Clinton proposals like health-care reform. In 1998, Gingrich was sure Monicagate made the lame-duck president a sitting duck as well. America disagreed. When the Republicans' edge was trimmed, the Speaker quit.

P. F. BENTLEY / TIME

PEACE IN THEIR TIME

Apartheid ended not with a bang but with this salute. In May 1994, Nelson Mandela, 75, was sworn in as South Africa's president and his predecessor, F. W. de Klerk, 58, as a deputy president. Four years earlier, de Klerk had freed Mandela after 27 years as a political prisoner. Their subsequent dialogue on black-white power sharing won them a joint Nobel — and their beloved country a multiracial future.

JUDA NGWENYA / REUTERS / ARCHIVE PHOTOS

CATASTROPHE IN OKLAHOMA

A federal office building in Oklahoma City was blown apart on April 19, 1995, by a truck bomb that killed 168 — among them, 19 tots in a child-care center — and injured 850. Terrorist Timothy McVeigh, 28, home-brewed the explosive from feed-store chemicals and highly flammable racing fuel. The Desert Storm veteran believed in the far-right radicalism of militiamen, survivalists and others. Oklahoma City was his answer to Waco, Texas, where, surrounded by federal agents, 75 members of survivalist David Koresh's cult had died on April 19, 1993. For his crime, McVeigh received the death penalty.

JIM ARGO / DAILY OKLAHOMAN / SABA

A City in the Clouds

Yale historian Hiram Bingham (who served as inspiration for the movie character Indiana Jones) was searching the Peruvian highlands for a legendary lost Inca city in 1911 when he came upon Machu Picchu. It was a key ceremonial center for the advanced civilization that ruled much of the Andes for 200-plus years before its 16th Century conquest, in just 40 years, by Spain.

Time Inc.

Dinner at Eight

Beginning with his dig at the Iraqi site of Ur in 1922, Leonard Woolley (right) reversed the cruel loot-and-run philosophy of fieldwork. The British archaeologist documented each find, no matter how small. Among his prizes from Ur: the inlaid panel below showing a royal banquet circa 2500 B.C., when the pre-Babylonian kingdom of Sumer ruled ancient Mesopotamia.

Right: Corbis / Bettmann

Below: Frank Scherschel / Life

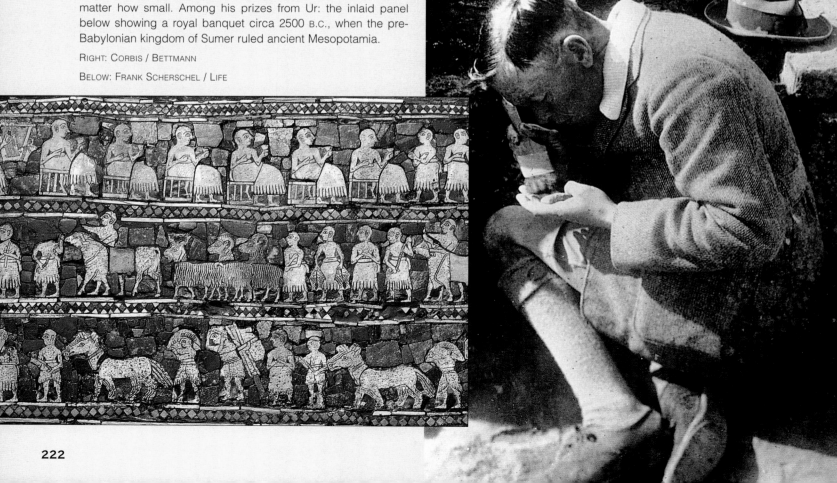

Our Family Tree

The past roars with things to tell us. We have begun to hear, thanks to 20th Century know-how. These days, a chip of bone, a carved rock, a petrified seed can be scanned like bar codes for date of origin. So we are able to push back ever further in our century-long search for the missing link, that changing species of primates evolving into *Homo sapiens*. We've also refound some long-lost kin. Guess what? Even the earliest bonded. And cocooned. And lit fires. And buried their dead. And made war — and art. Which is to say, they stopped dragging their knuckles much earlier than we so smugly thought. How's this for a notion: We'd be hardly more awkward around a native of way-back-when than we are visiting a country where the natives speak a different tongue.

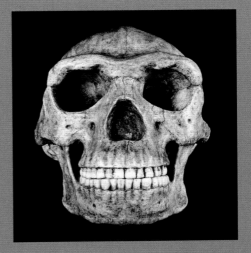

LONG-LOST RELATIVE

From 1927 on, paleontologists began to find, in caves near Peking, a trove of skeletal remains more than 400,000 years old. They also unearthed tools and singed animal bones. Strikingly identical to modern humans from the neck down, Peking Man had not much of a forehead. (Its brain averaged four-fifths the size of ours.) The original specimens vanished during the 1941 Japanese invasion of China; more have since been discovered.

AMERICAN MUSEUM OF NATURAL HISTORY

PRESENT AT THE CREATION

Two millennia ago, near Khirbat Qumran by the Dead Sea, a clay urn (top, after restoration) containing some leather scrolls was placed in a cave. It was found in 1947 by young Bedouins. Though the leather had split (inset), the Hebraic script was legible. The scrolls (plus others found nearby) were worth deciphering: The texts give a firsthand look, from the epicenter, of the emergence of Christianity from its Judaic roots.

CORBIS / BETTMANN-UPI

INSET: LARRY BURROWS / LIFE

ETERNAL COMPANIONS

In 1974 farmers digging for water near Xi'an in northwest China struck historical gold: an imperial tomb filled with 6,000 bronze horses and life-size terra-cotta warriors (each with a unique face), and more. Shih Huang-ti deserved the royal send-off; he had ordered work begun on a wall that would eventually stretch 1,500 miles across China.

EASTFOTO / XINHUA NEWS AGENCY

SURROGATE PARENTS

The hands-and-knees patience of British fossil hunters Louis and Mary Leakey yielded, in 1959, skull chips that forced a major revision of evolutionary theory. The fragments were of a tool-using hominid who lived 1.75 million years ago in Tanzania's Olduvai Gorge; later finds pushed our earliest two-legged ancestors back to 4.4 million B.C.

NGS IMAGE COLLECTION

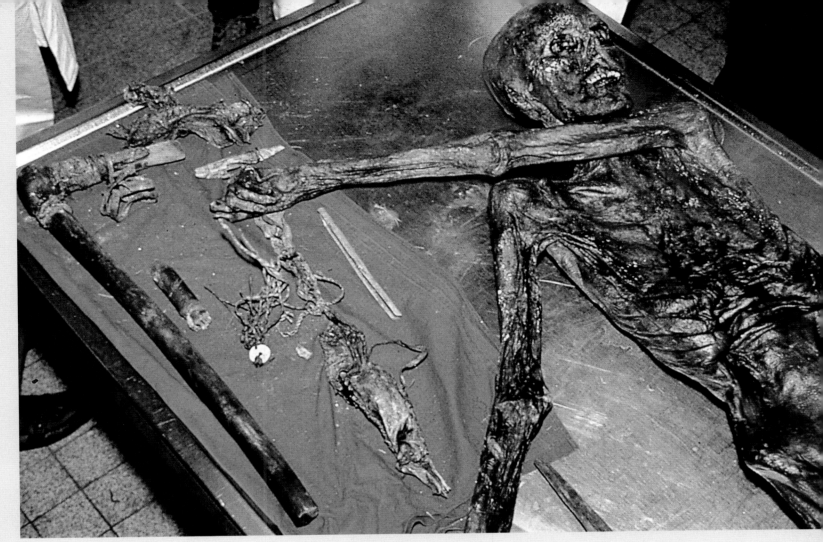

FROZEN IN TIME

One day 5,300 years ago a man of about 30, above, was crossing the Tyrolean Alps when overtaken by a blizzard. His icy tomb did not thaw until 1991. So well preserved was he that we know his eye color (blue) and basic diet (milled grains). We also learned that in the Stone Age, some guys cut their hair short and sported tattoos.

GERHARD HINTERLEITNER / LIAISON

THE FIRST PICTURE SHOW

Late in 1994, three French cave explorers became the first visitors to an underground gallery in 30,000 years. The cave paintings at Vallon-Pont-d'Arc in southeastern France are more sophisticated than those of the Lascaux Grotto (done 17,000 years later). Of the images, 415 are of animals — and one of a bison whose legs are clearly human.

JEAN CLOTTES / SYGMA

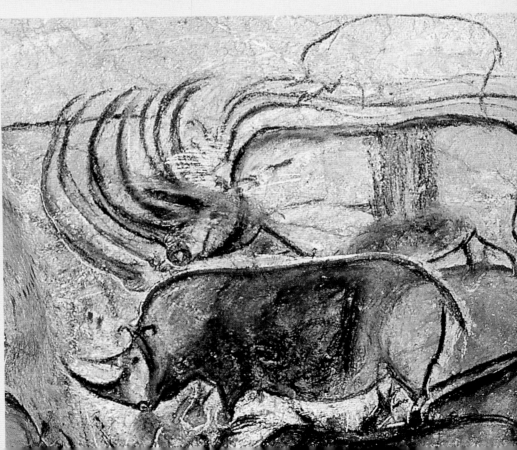

AIR JORDAN

→

Michael Jordan, unlike Alexander the Great, retired when he had no worlds left to conquer. He led the Chicago Bulls to six titles in the last eight years of his 13-year basketball career and scored 29,277 points. So in early 1999 (with wife Juanita's O.K., as long as no more baseball), he rejected $21.2 million and went about his businesses. If Michael, 35, looked choked up, consider the NBA: It had no Air apparent.

JOHN BIEVER / SPORTS ILLUSTRATED

A NEW CHASE BEGINS

Thirty-seven seasons after their dad hit a benchmark 61 home runs, Kevin Maris, 38 (far left), and brother Roger Jr., 39, greeted Mark McGwire, who had just nailed number 62. It was a year for going yard. Chicago Cub Sammy Sosa finished 1998 with 66 home runs, but McGwire, 34, outbashed him by four.

JOHN BIEVER / SPORTS ILLUSTRATED

→ HOMOPHOBIA ON THE RANGE

Lured from a bar in Laramie, Wyoming, a gay college student was roped to this fence in October 1998 after being beaten, burned and robbed. Matthew Shepard, 21, was barely alive when found after 18 hours. He died five days later.

STEVE LISS / TIME

GRRRL POWER!

As Brazil's Pelé ruled men's soccer a third of a century ago, so America's Mia Hamm, 27, has dominated the rising women's game. The Air Force brat was also the most visible beneficiary of Title IX, a law enacted three months after her birth that required colleges to fund women's sports. Hamm led Team USA to the packed 1999 Women's World Cup finals. They won.

CHUCK SOLOMON / SPORTS ILLUSTRATED

→ NO PLACE LIKE HOME

Welcoming a U.N. peace-keeper to Kosovo province in Yugoslavia in June 1999 was no stretch for these kids; restoring their lives would be. They and fellow Albanians had been targeted for "ethnic cleansing" (killing) by Belgrade. It was the latest sad chapter of a seven-year, religion-fueled civil war ruining the nation that had hosted 1984's sparkling Winter Games at Sarajevo.

YANNIS BEHRAKIS / REUTERS / ARCHIVE PHOTOS

→
ARTHUR ASHE
1943–1993

In 1968, he became the last amateur and first black to win the U.S. Open men's singles. When heart disease cut short his tennis career, Ashe took up an activism inspired by having to learn the game on segregated courts in Richmond, Virginia. To civil rights he would add championing other victims of AIDS, which he had contracted through a tainted blood transfusion.

JOHN ZIMMERMAN / LIFE

↑
CESAR CHAVEZ
1927–1993

He taught Anglo-Americans the word *huelga,* or strike. Born in Yuma, Arizona, to migrant workers, he himself was a stoop laborer except for a Navy stint during World War II. In 1965, Chavez began a strike against California grape growers that was won in 1970. He soon organized other agricultural workers and, in 1977, even took on the Teamsters Union — and beat them.

BILL EPPRIDGE / LIFE

←
WILMA RUDOLPH
1940–1994

First she outran polio. Then she outran an impoverished childhood in rural Tennessee. In 1960, at the Rome Olympics, she outran the competition in the 100- and 200-meters, as well as in the sprint relay, to become the first American woman to win three golds at one Games. After hanging up her spikes, Rudolph worked in inner cities, showing kids the fastest way out.

MARK KAUFFMAN / LIFE

→
JERRY GARCIA
1942–1995

In Jerry's 30 years fronting the band, the Grateful Dead lived on tour, giving free-form concerts — powered by his extended guitar jams — that left fans glassy-eyed. Even those who were clean. Cherry Garcia was a witty name for an ice cream flavor, though he probably preferred Heavenly Hash. Garcia never did kick his drug habit; he was in rehab when the heart attack hit.

HENRY GROSSMAN

JOHN F. KENNEDY JR.
1960–1999

Born two months before his family moved into the White House, the child spent his third birthday helping bury a dad he hardly knew. Kennedy did not enter politics despite his bloodlines and an appearance of personal glamour. Instead, he co-founded a public affairs magazine. En route to a cousin's wedding, the plane he was piloting crashed; on board were wife Carolyn, 33 (right), and sister-in-law Lauren Bessette.

REQUIEM

MOTHER TERESA
1910–1997

Along with a healer's hand, she had a fund-raiser's gift for publicizing her empire of charity (here, with Princess Diana in 1997). At 18, Agnes Gonxha Bojaxhiu was sent by a Catholic order to India. Twenty years later, she and her nuns began to tend the leprous, the maimed, the dying. By the time Mother Teresa won a 1979 Nobel, she oversaw 250 centers worldwide.

DIANA, PRINCESS OF WALES
1961–1997

At age 19, she accepted the proposal of a prince of the realm. We watched her every move from that day forward. Princess Diana's death in August 1997, at 36, in a Paris traffic accident, focused the world on London, where floral tributes flooded Kensington Palace and her funeral procession passed an estimated two million people.

INDEX

A

Allen, Paul, 199
Andrews, Julie, 32
Anne, Princess, 135
Anthony, Susan B., 21
Arafat, Yasir, 218
Armstrong, Louis, 48
Armstrong, Neil, 174
Arnaz, Desi, 134
Ashe, Arthur, 228
Aykroyd, Dan, 181

B

Baez, Joan, 152
Baker, Kenny, 190
Ball, Lucille, 134
Bannister, Roger, 142
Barbie doll, 144
Bar-Lev, Haim, 173
Barrow, Clyde, 76
Begin, Menachem, 190
Bell, Alexander Graham, 63
Belushi, John, 181
Bernstein, Leonard, 32 (West Side Story)
Bicentennial, 184–85
Bikini, 131
Bird, Larry, 195
Bolger, Ray, 84
Borden, Lizzie, 62
Braun, Eva, 98
Brown, Linda, 138
Brown, Louise, 192
Brownie camera, 9
Bryan, William Jennings, 58

C

Capone, Al, 77
Capra, Frank, 85 (Mr. Smith Goes to Washington)
Carnegie, Andrew, 43
Carpenter, Scott, 174
Carter, Howard, 50
Carter, Jimmy, 190
Caruso, Enrico, 63
Carver, George Washington, 119
Castro, Fidel, 148
Challenger, 177
Chamberlain, Wilt, 153
Charles, Prince, 135, 196
Chase, Chevy, 181
Chavez, Cesar, 228
Checker, Chubby, 149
Chernobyl, 117
Child laborer, 14
Chisholm, Shirley, 54
Chou En-Lai, 79
Churchill, Winston, 108, 120
Civil defense drill, 116
Civil disorder, 164 (Watts), 164–65 (Detroit), 170 (Paris), 170 (1968 Chicago Democratic National Convention), 208 (Los Angeles)
Civil rights, 125, 138 (Selma), 139
Civil war, 194 (Afghanistan), 199 (El Salvador), 219 (Rwanda), 227 (Yugoslavia)
Clark, Dick, 143
Clay, Cassius (Muhammad Ali), 162
Clemente, Roberto, 182
Clinton, Bill, 207, 217, 218
Cody, William F., 42
Cold War, 127 (Berlin airlift), 149 (Berlin Wall begun), 151 (Cuban Missile Crisis), 170 (Prague Spring)
Comaneci, Nadia, 188
Cooper, Gordon, 174
Cosby, Bill, 201
Crick, Francis, 136
Curie, Marie and Pierre, 115
Curtin, Jane, 181

D

Dalai Lama, 81
Daniels, Anthony, 190
Dead Sea Scrolls, 223
Dean, James, 155
Dean, John, 178
De Gaulle, Charles, 147
De Klerk, F. W., 221
Desert Storm, 196, 204
Diana, Princess of Wales, 196, 229
DiCaprio, Leonardo, 19
Didrickson, Babe, 70
DiMaggio, Joe, 112
Disney, Walt, 58
Dolly the sheep, 212–13
Dr. Seuss (Theodore Geisel), 209
Du Bois, W. E. B., 139
Dylan, Bob, 152

E

Earhart, Amelia, 88
Earp, Wyatt, 62
Ederle, Gertrude, 49
Edison, Thomas Alva, 88
Einstein, Albert, 115
Eisenhower, Dwight D., 105
Elizabeth II, Queen, 135
Ellington, Duke, 112
Ellis Island, 17
Empire State Building, 59
Evans, John, 170
Exxon Valdez, 202

F

Faldo, Nick, 216
Ferdinand, Archduke Franz, 25 (with Duchess Sophie)
Fermi, Enrico, 114
Ferraro, Geraldine, 55
Fitzgerald, F. Scott, 118 (with wife Zelda)
Ford car, 15 (Model T), 114 (Thunderbird)
Ford, Gerald, 179 (with wife Betty)
Ford, Henry, 15
Franco, Francisco, 80
Frank, Anne, 126
Frawley, William, 134
Freud, Sigmund, 89
Frost, Robert, 154

G

Gable, Clark, 85
Gagarin, Yuri, 150
Gandhi, Mohandas, 129
Garcia, Jerry, 229
Garland, Judy, 84
Garner, John Nance, 71
Gates, Bill, 199
Gay, Margie, 58
Gehrig, Lou, 118
Geronimo, 20
Gershwin, George, 89
Gibson, Althea, 145
Gillespie, Vernon, 163
Gingrich, Newt, 220
Glenn, John, 174
Goddard, Robert, 175
Gorman, Margaret, 44
Gotti, John, 77
Graham, Martha, 113
Great Depression, 64–65 (Dust Bowl), 69, 72, 74–75 (Dust Bowl)
Grissom, Gus, 174
Groves, Leslie, 114
Guevara, Ernesto (Che), 182
Guthrie, Woody, 182

H

Haley, Jack, 84
Hamm, Mia, 227
Hammerstein, Oscar, II, 32 (Oklahoma!), 33 (Show Boat)
Hare Krishnas, 167
Harlem Hellfighters, 40
Harrison, George, 152
Harrison, Rex, 32
Hearst, Patty, 180
Heisler, Gregory, 220
Henson, Jim, 211
Hillary, Edmund, 136
Hindenburg, 80
Hitchcock, Alfred, 211
Hitler, Adolf, 86–87 (at Nuremberg rally), 98
Hoff, Charles, 56
Holiday, Billie, 154
Holocaust, 102, 108
Hoover, J. Edgar, 68
Hula Hoop, 146

I

Iran, 193
Ireland, 30 (Easter Monday)

Iron lung machine, 83
Israel, 128, 166 (Six Day War)

J

Jackson, Joe, 39
Jackson, Michael, 200
Jefferson, Joseph, 8
John Paul II, Pope, 198
Johns, Jasper, 142
Johnson, Earvin (Magic), 195
Jones, Bobby, 61
Jonestown, Guyana, 192
Joplin, Janis, 172
Jordan, Michael, 226 (with wife Juanita)

K

Keller, Helen, 8
Kelly, Grace, 144
Kemp, G. S., 9
Kennedy, John F., 150, 153
Kennedy, John F., Jr., 229 (with wife Carolyn)
Kennedy, Robert F., 169
Kern, Jerome, 33 *(Show Boat)*
Khrushchev, Nikita, 150, 162 (with wife Nina)
King, Billie Jean Moffitt, 129
King, Larry, 205
King, Martin Luther, Jr., 140–41, 170
Korean War, 132–33
Kubrick, Stanley, 158 *(Dr. Strangelove)*
Ku Klux Klan, 138

L

Labor unions, U.S., 82
Lahr, Bert, 84
Larson, Jonathan, 32 *(Rent)*
Laughlin, T. P., 35
Leaky, Lewis, 224
Leaky, Mary, 224
Leigh, Vivien, 85
Lenin, Vladimir, 40
Lennon, John, 159, 209
Lerner, Alan Jay, 32 *(My Fair Lady)*
Lewinsky, Monica, 217
Lindbergh, Charles, 51
Lindbergh, Charles, Jr., 72
Littleton, Colorado, massacre, 215
Loan, Nguyen Ngoc, 168
Loewe, Frederick, 32 *(My Fair Lady)*
Longbaugh, Harry, 76 (Sundance Kid)
Lop, Bay, 168
Lucas, George, 190 *(Star Wars)*

M

MacArthur, Douglas, 108, 111
Machu Picchu, 222
Madonna, 189
Malcolm X, 164 (with wife Betty Shabazz and daughters)
Maltby, Richard, Jr., 33 *(Ain't Misbehavin')*
Mandela, Nelson, 221
Manson, Charles, 173
Mao Tse-tung, 79, 165 (Cultural Revolution)
Marconi, Guglielmo, 9
Maris, Kevin and Roger, Jr., 226
Marley, Bob, 208
Marshall, George, 127
Marshall, Thurgood, 141 (with wife Cecilia)
McCandless, Bruce, 176

McCarthy, Joseph, 137
McCartney, Paul, 152
McDaniels, Darryl, 201
McDonald's, 124
McGwire, Mark, 226
McKinley, William, 4
Mead, Margaret, 210
Meir, Golda, 173
Milken, Michael, 202
Miller, Arthur, 145
Miller, Jeffrey, 161
Miss America pageant, 44–45
Mizell, Jason, 201
Molotov, V. M., 87
Mondale, Walter, 55
Monroe, Marilyn, 145
Morgan, J. P., 5 (with children)
Morris, Garrett, 181
Muir, John, 42
Mussolini, Benito, 78

N

Naismith, James, 88
Newman, Laraine, 181
New York City, 13 (El)
NFL Championship, 146 (1958)
Nicholas II, Czar, 6 (with Alexandra), 34 (with family)
Nightingale, Florence, 21
Nixon, Richard M., 171, 178
Norgay, Tenzing, 136
Norris, Clarence, 70
Nuclear weapon, 116 (first A-bomb)

O

Oakley, Annie, 62
Oberon, Merle, 84
O'Connor, Sandra Day, 55
O'Keeffe, Georgia, 208
Olivier, Laurence, 84
Onassis, Jacqueline Kennedy, 153
Oppenheimer, J. Robert, 114
Oswald, Lee Harvey, 153
Owens, Jesse, 68
Ozone layer, 202

P

Panama Canal, 17
Parker, Bonnie, 76
Parker, Robert, 76 (Butch Cassidy)
Parks, Rosa, 139
Paul, Alice, 53
Peking Man, 223
Pepe, Maria, 180
Perkins, Frances, 53
Perón, Eva, 154
Perot, Ross, 205
Petersen, Hector, 191
Picasso, Pablo, 12 *(Les Demoiselles d'Avignon)*
Pill, 147 (birth control)
Postcolonial independence, 148 (Algeria)
Potter, Beatrix, 119
Powell, Colin, 141 (with wife Alma)
Presley, Elvis, 142
Prohibition, 47, 73 (repeal of)
Protest demonstration, 52 (women's suffrage), 156–57 (Kent State), 159 (Vietnam War), 161 (Kent State), 173 (pro-choice)
Pulliam, Keshia Knight, 201

Q

Queen, H. L., 82

R

Rabin, Yitzhak, 218
Radner, Gilda, 181
Ranier III, Prince, 144
Rankin, Jeannette, 53
Reagan, Ronald, 198
Renoir, Pierre-Auguste, 42
Ribbentrop, Joachim von, 87
Rickenbacker, Eddie, 35
Robbins, Jerome, 32 *(West Side Story)*
Robinson, Jackie, 128
Rockefeller, John D., 88 (with son)
Rodgers, Richard, 32 *(Oklahoma!)*
Roosevelt, Eleanor, 93
Roosevelt, Franklin D., 53, 71, 108, 196
Roosevelt, Theodore, 4 (with family)
Rose Bowl, 8
Rosenberg, Ethel and Julius, 136
Ruby, Jack, 153
Rudolph, Wilma, 228
Russian Revolution, 31
Ruth, Babe, 60

S

Sacco, Nicola, 50
Sadat, Anwar, 190
Salk, Jonas, 123
San Francisco Earthquake of 1906, 12
Sanger, Margaret, 30
Schindler, Oskar, 183
Schirra, Wally, 174
Schwarzkopf, Norman, 204
Scott, Robert, 16
Scottsboro Boys, 70
Sellers, Peter, 158
Shepard, Alan, 174
Shepard, Matthew, 227
Shih Huang-ti, 224 (tomb)
Simmons, Joseph, 201
Simpson, O. J., 197
Sinatra, Frank, 112 (with family)
Slayton, Deke, 174
Smith, E. J., 19
Smith, Margaret Chase, 54
Soupart, Pierre, 192
South Africa, 131, 191 (Soweto), 197
Space exploration, 147 (laika), 161, 175, 176, 177
Spanish flu epidemic of 1918, 38
Spielberg, Steven, 200 *(E.T.)*
Stalin, Joseph, 79, 87, 108, 136
Starr, Ringo, 152
Stevens, Tempest, 57
Stewart, James, 85
Stolley, Dick, vii
Straus, Isador and Ida, 18
Suburbia, 131
Sullivan, Anne, 8
Summer of Love, 167

T

Temple, Shirley, 67
Teresa, Mother, 229
Terra Nova, 16
Terrorism, 215 (Unabomber), 218 (Tokyo subways), 218 (World Trade Center), 221 (Oklahoma City)

Thatcher, Margaret, 187
Thomas, Henry, 200
Thorpe, Jim, 155
Tiananmen Square, 203
Titanic, 3, 18–19
Tobacco industry, 220
Tojo, Hideki, 126
Tolkien, J. R. R., 183
Triangle Shirtwaist Fire, 15
Trotsky, Leon, 81 (with wife Natalia)
Truman, Harry S, 120 (with family)
Tubman, Harriet, 20
Turner, Ted, 196
Tutankhamen, 50
TV dinner, 134
Twain, Mark, 21
Tz'u-Hsi, Empress Dowager, 6

U
Ur, 222

V
Vallon-Pont-d'Arc, 225 (cave paintings)
Vance, Vivian, 134
Vanzetti, Bartolomeo, 50
Vecchio, Mary Ann, 161
Victoria, Queen, 7
Vietnam War, 160, 163, 168 (Tet Offensive, My Lai)
Villa, Pancho, 31

W
Walesa, Lech, 193
Warhol, Andy, 150 (*Campbell's Soup Can, 19¢*)
Warren, Earl, 183
Washington, Booker T., 43
Watergate hearings, 178
Watson, James, 136
Weissmuller, Johnny, 61
Welch, Joseph, 137
Williams, Tennessee, 210
Wilson, Woodrow, 41
Winfrey, Oprah, 201
Winslet, Kate, 19
Woods, Tiger, 216
Woodstock, 172
Woolley, Leonard, 222
Woolworth, Frank, 42
World War I, 22–23 (Mons), 26, 28, 29 (Gallipoli), 36–37, 40
World War II, 90–91, 96 (Blitz of London), 97, 99 (Pearl Harbor), 100 (Bataan), 101 (Battle of Midway), 101 (Guadalcanal), 102, 103, 104–05 (D-Day), 106 (Battle of the Bulge), 107 (kamikaze), 107 (Iwo Jima), 110 (Hiroshima), 111
World War II, U.S. homefront, 94, 109 (V-E Day), 111 (V-J Day)
Wright, Frank Lloyd, 154
Wright, Orville, 10, 11
Wright, Wilbur, 10, 11

Y
Yeager, Chuck, 127
Yeltsin, Boris, 205

EXTENDED PICTURE CREDITS

While every effort has been made to give appropriate credit for photographs and illustrations reproduced in this book, the publishers will be pleased to rectify any omissions or inaccuracies in the next printing.

Page ii: NASA
Page 4, bottom right: S0117495, 40-12-05/10, color transparency. Brazille, Frédéric (1841–1870). Pierre Auguste Renoir, painter. Oil on canvas, 1867. 62 x 51 cm. Musée d'Orsay, Paris, France.
Page 12, top: Steinbrugge Collection, Earthquake Engineering Research Center, University of California, Berkeley.
Page 12, bottom: Picasso, Pablo. Les Demoiselles d'Avignon. Paris (June–July 1907). Oil on canvas, 8′ by 7′8″ (243.9 by 233.7 cm). The Museum of Modern Art, New York. Acquired through the Lillie P. Bliss Bequest. Photograph, 1999, The Museum of Modern Art, New York.
Page 13: Millstein Division of U.S. History, Local History & Genealogy, The New York Public Library, Astor, Lenox and Tilden Foundations.
Page 15: Brown Brothers.
Page 17, right: Millstein Division of U.S. History, Local History & Genealogy, The New York Public Library, Astor, Lenox and Tilden Foundations.
Page 50, bottom: Photography by Egyptian Expedition, The Metropolitan Museum of Art.
Page 59: Romana Javitz Collection, Miriam and Ira D. Wallach Division of Arts, Prints and Photographs, The New York Public Library, Astor, Lenox and Tilden Foundations.
Page 80, top: Dever / Black Star.
Page 89, left: Reprinted with permission of Joanna T. Steichen.
Page 127, top: Harry Ransom Humanities Research Center, Photography Collection, The University of Texas at Austin.
Page 150, bottom: S0114138, OC54.002, color transparency. Warhol, Andy (1928–1987). Campbell's Soup Can, 19¢, 1962. Synthetic polymer paint and silkscreen ink and graphite on canvas; 72 by 54 inches.
Page 223, right: AMNH negative #315447, courtesy Department of Library Services, American Museum of Natural History.

LIFE: Our Century in Pictures For Young People

Editor: Richard B. Stolley
Adapter: Amy E. Sklansky
Writer: Tony Chiu
Picture Editor: Debra Cohen
Researcher: Carol Weil
Copyeditor: Steve Lamont
Mechancial layout: Alicia Cech

Special thanks to Sheilah Scully, Ellen Graham, Gretchen Wessels (photo researchers), Pamela Wilson, Annette Rusin, Brenda Cherry (researchers), Sally Proudfit, Bob Jackson, Helene Veret, and Jennifer McAlwee.

Produced in cooperation with Time Inc. Editorial Services

Director: Sheldon Czapnik
Research Center: Lany McDonald
Picture Collection:
    Beth Iskander, Kathi Doak
Photo Lab: Tom Hubbard
Time-Life Syndication:
    Maryann Kornely

LIFE Magazine
Managing Editor: Isolde Motley
Publisher: Donald B. Fries

Published by Time Warner Trade Publishing
Chairman, Time Warner Trade Publishing:
    Laurence J. Kirshbaum
Publisher, Little, Brown and Company Children's Books: John G. Keller
Editor, Little, Brown and Company Children's Books: Cynthia Eagan
Production Manager, Little, Brown and Company Children's Books: Linda Jackson
Art Director/Designer, Little, Brown and Company Children's Books: Sheila Smallwood

First Edition
This book is based on *LIFE: Our Century in Pictures* (Bulfinch Press, 1999) and features photographs from that book.

Library of Congress Cataloging-in-Publication Data
Life: our century in pictures for young people / edited by Richard B. Stolley ; adapted by Amy E. Sklansky — 1st ed.
p. cm.
"This book is based on Life: our century in pictures (Bulfinch Press, 1999) and features photographs from that book." — T.p. verso.
Includes index.
ISBN 0-316-81589-6
ISBN 0-316-81577-2 (Scholastic ed.)
1. Twentieth century — Pictorial works — Juvenile literature. 2. Civilization, Modern — 20th century — Juvenile literature.
    [1. Civilization, Modern — 20th century.
    2. Twentieth century.] I. Stolley, Richard B. II. Sklansky, Amy E. III. Life (New York, N.Y.) IV. Life.
CB426 .L54 2000
909.82 — dc21   00-032877

Printed in the U.S.A.